Wayne Goddard's
$50 Knife Shop
REVISED

Get Started Without Spending a Fortune

Published by

Krause Publications, a division of F+W, A Content + eCommerce Company
700 East State Street • Iola, WI 54990-0001
715-445-2214 • 888-457-2873
www.krausebooks.com

To order books or other products call toll-free 1-800-258-0929
or visit us online at www.krausebooks.com or www.shopblade.com

Library of Congress Control Number: 2005906860

ISBN 10-digit: 0-89689-295-6
ISBN 13-digit: 978-0-89689-295-8

Designed by Kara Grundman
Edited by Kevin Michalowski

Printed in the United States of America

ACKNOWLEDGEMENTS

I thank God for giving me an inquisitive mind. I thank Phyllis for her love, devotion and support; she made my career as a knifemaker possible. I could not have done it working alone. It wouldn't have been possible for me to learn knifemaking and support my family at the same time. Phyllis worked so that we could pay the bills and have health insurance. She was a working partner in the knife business even though she wasn't in the shop with me. Thank you, Honey.

The pioneers of the modern handmade knife era made it easier for those of us who followed the trails they blazed. The knifemaker who had the most impact on my career was Bob Loveless. I was getting ready to go into knifemaking full time during 1971-1972 and Bob was never too busy to answer all my questions. I attended my first Knifemakers' Guild show in 1972 and found Bob as supportive in person as he was over the phone and by mail. I appreciated his no nonsense and practical approach to knives and what they were about.

His purity of design and clean workmanship gave me a goal to strive for. Bob was always a leader in finding new and improved blade materials. A lot of the excitement and growth of the handmade knife world in those early years came from his introduction of 154-CM. Thanks, Bob.

Wayne Goddard
January 2006

It takes practice and hard work, not fancy tools to make a great-looking knife like this.

TABLE OF CONTENTS

INTRODUCTION
The $50 Knife Shop............................5

CHAPTER 1
Knifemaking Simplified.....................6

CHAPTER 2
The Forged Knife............................20

CHAPTER 3
The Stock-Removal Method and Finishing....48

CHAPTER 4
Backyard Heat Treating.....................70

CHAPTER 5
Primitive Knifemaking 90

CHAPTER 6
Damascus Steel.............................104

CHAPTER 7
Homemade Grinders 122

CHAPTER 8
Jigs, Fixtures And Holding Devices
For The Knife Shop 142

THE $50 KNIFE SHOP

Back in 1988, I took on a project that was printed in Dixie Gun Works' 1988 Blackpowder Annual. The plan was to make a forged buckskinner knife with a minimum of equipment. For that project, I built an anvil out of railroad rail, made a coal forge from a rusted-out barbecue and finished the knife by hand without the use of any power tools.

That project helped to spawn *The $50 Knife Shop* series for *BLADE® Magazine*. The column was actually an expansion on my earlier experiments. It was a reaction to the "high-tech" methods that are being used to create hand-made knives today. I'm not saying there is anything wrong with using technology and machine tools to their fullest extent. What I am saying is that high-tech it is not for everyone and this book is for those who want to simplify the process. Although the equipment is simple and low-cost, a high-quality knife can be made. It truly is possible to set up to both forge and grind knives and keep the budget under $50. The main requirement is having the desire to do it; I call it having the want-to's.

In the pages that follow I will be teaching my way through the two project knives that were finished in the magazine series. Along the way there will be some side trips to cover in-depth the things that there wasn't space for in the magazine series.

The Forged Project

The magazine series started out with forging because it requires a minimum of tools to get a finished knife. The "World's Smallest Forge" was used for forging the blade. The forged-to-shape blade was cleaned up with files and then hand-rubbed on "wet-rocks" made from broken sandstone grinding wheels to get it smooth enough for heat treatment. That was in keeping with the aim to use no power tools in the making of the forged blade. In order to keep the budget down; I used a tree branch from my dad's yard for the handle.

The Stock-Removal Project

For this knife, I went back to 1963 and my start in knifemaking by constructing a faithful reproduction of

my first grinder. It was made from a washing machine motor and some other junk. I used an abrasive saw on my reproduction grinder to cut a lawnmower blade into blanks. I then put a grinding wheel on it to shape the profile and grind the bevels. I used a disc sanding attachment on an electric drill to smooth it up and get it ready for heat treatment. I used a propane-torch to heat the one-brick forge. I used the "goop" quench to harden the two blades. Blades were tempered in a toaster oven. Scrap maple burl was used for the handle slabs on the stock-removal blade. That's about as simple as it can get.

The Bottom Line

I started the magazine series with the assumption that I could make both the forged and stock-removal project for $50. I came in under budget, at least on paper. The following is a list of the materials and equipment that it took to complete the series.

Coal forge	$5
Makeshift anvil and forge tools	$10
The Good News, Bad News Grinder	$5
1955 Black and Decker Drill	$2
Drill press adapter	Free
Toaster oven	$2
World's Smallest Forge	$10
Blade and handle material for two knives	$2
Total	$36

At the end of the series I made the comment that I should use the leftover $14 to build a belt grinder. I missed my estimate by $2; the final cost of the 1 by 42 belt grinder was built for $16 worth of yard sale parts. You'll find the details on it in the section on homemade grinders.

So then, we are about to undertake a couple projects that should teach you about knifemaking on a budget. The figure of $50 is really arbitrary. It is the philosophy of working with the tools you have or can acquire inexpensively that's really important. If you really want to, you can create a serviceable knife shop for a lot less than you think.

CHAPTER 1

KNIFEMAKING SIMPLIFIED

There is a well-known knifemaker who tells newcomers that an investment of $20,000 is necessary to fund a fully equipped shop. I can't disagree with that, however that shop will not make anyone a knifemaker. On the other hand, if a lot of tools were truly necessary, I and most of the makers who started in the 1960s and 1970s would never have made our first knives.

The backyard smithy, 1988.

The coal forge made from a rusted out barbecue. A piece of Honda automobile spring, a flattened section on one piece, a pre-form on the other.

It's a fact that knifemakers shops get more "high-tech" all the time. There are those individuals who want, and perhaps need to have all the latest and best machinery. There is nothing wrong with that. It's just not necessary for the beginner. Without a lot of practice a room full of expensive tools won't make anyone a knifemaker. It will take months, perhaps years for the new maker to become skillful enough to be competitive in the marketplace. I'm convinced that the best way to start any new enterprise is with simple equipment. If the fundamentals can't be learned with simple tools and methods it may not be possible to learn it with more "high-tech" equipment. The cold, hard facts are that the latest and best technology will not replace years of practice with simple tools.

It's often discouraging for a would-be knifemaker to see a well-equipped shop. A simple beginning does not appeal to most folks once they have seen my shop full of machinery and tools. They usually think everything they see is necessary in order to make knives. I heard this comment once, "I won't be able to make knives, I can't afford all this stuff!" My stuff makes me more efficient and better prepared to support myself as a knifemaker. It certainly isn't necessary to get started.

I like to tell people about the small table that held all my equipment when I moved to my present location in 1969. I tell them how I made more than 300 knives before I had a belt grinder. I explain that it has taken me

more than 42 years to accumulate all that I have. Once they see all my stuff, the damage is often done. Building a homemade grinder and setting up shop under a shade tree in their backyard is not how they visualize the knifemaking process.

I sometimes hear the excuse; "My knives would be better if I had better equipment." I have sad news for those folks. Machines don't come with whatever it takes to develop the skill to do good work. Regardless of the equipment, it will take many hours and days of practice to develop the skill necessary to do good work. I've seen more than a few new makers who had the dollars to obtain good equipment but then became frustrated by their insufficient skill to do good work with their tools.

Another excuse I sometimes hear is, "I want to make knives but don't have the time." People generally spend their time on what is most interesting to them at the time. It's a matter of priorities and if they have a genuine desire and sufficient knowledge they will make time for knifemaking.

Some people don't stick with knifemaking long enough to master it. Success usually comes to those who never give up. The most important ingredient for success with simple methods is to have a sincere desire to do it.

In order to teach the stock-removal method on a simple basis I went back to the way I started in 1963. The forged knife section of the series came out of my experiments started in 1984 to make knives without any power equipment. My success with that project proved that the desire to make knives is the only necessary ingredient for the would-be knifemaker. Those two facets of my career came together in the *BLADE® Magazine* series *The $50 Knife Shop*. The first edition of this book grew out of that series and this, the second edition, grew out of the results.

No excuses now, it's time to get to work.

A Talent For Knifemaking

There may be such a thing as a "talent" for making knives. I didn't have it when I started and I can prove it. There's a sheet-metal box in my shop with a couple dozen knives in it that I made in the 1960s and 1970s. Whenever someone tries to tell me I have a talent for making knives I show them the knives from those early years. I've heard comments like "How could you have done that!" My excuse is that I didn't know any better. I didn't have the talent for it and had never seen any well-made knives so I didn't have anything to work up to. My equipment was crude but I can't blame the knives on it. With the skill I

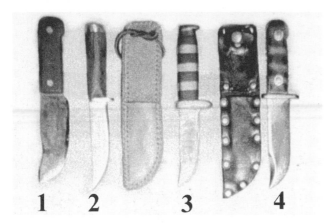

Group of knives by the author from 1963-1964.

The $50 Knife Shop in 2005.

The author at work in the original $50 Knife Shop.

Top, the project knife from the 1988 article, "How to Make a Buckskinner Knife". At center is the stock removal knife made from the worn out lawn mower blade. Bottom, the forged knife from The $50 Knife Shop series.

have today I can make first-class knives with very little in the way of tools. My opinion is that hard work, using good methods, develops skill. Talent may help if you are lucky enough to have it.

Teaching and Learning

I have a friend who tried to make a knife in another maker's shop but he wasn't getting anywhere with the blade. The teacher finally said, "… You don't have what it takes" and threw the blade away. I don't quite understand that attitude. It might be that the knifemaker/teacher had talent when he started to the extent that he didn't have to work at developing skill. He must have assumed that training wasn't really necessary if you had the talent. You either had it or didn't have it and he wasn't going to take the time to be a good teacher.

I've always said that anyone could learn to make knives. As I get older I have modified my statement to read like this. Anyone with the sincere desire can learn to make knives. My students come from all walks of life; dentists, loggers, crane operators, game wardens, roofers, welders, schoolteachers, physicians, and, no kidding, a butcher and a baker but no candlestick maker. Age is no barrier, my youngest student was 9, and the oldest was 81.

If you want to learn the most about knifemaking, start teaching. Teaching forces an individual to get under the surface of methods and techniques. Ask yourself these questions. Why is a certain style of knife shaped the way it is? Which handle shape works best for a specific blade shape? What does the relationship of the handle to the blade have on function? Why does one blade cut so much better than the next? What is balance? Finding the answers to these questions and a whole lot more is where the true rewards of knifemaking are found. Teach your kids, neighbors or friends. You'll be amazed at how much your knifemaking improves as you learn the deeper aspects of the craft. And, the competition will do you good.

Learning From Our Mistakes

I was in the middle of a project that didn't work out when a friend dropped in for a visit. Seeing the mess I was in, he was feeling sorry for me because of the time he thought I had wasted. I told him that I'd never be able to figure out what worked without first eliminating all the ideas that didn't work. The inventor who makes something work the first time is either very wise or just lucky. Either way, many valuable lessons were missed by not getting the experience of making something that didn't work.

The human eye can judge the difference between millions of different colors; this is a gift from our creator. The hand can make adjustments of a fraction of a degree and return to a previous angle, all without really

The author's first knife, made in 1963 using the makeshift grinder made from a washing machine motor.

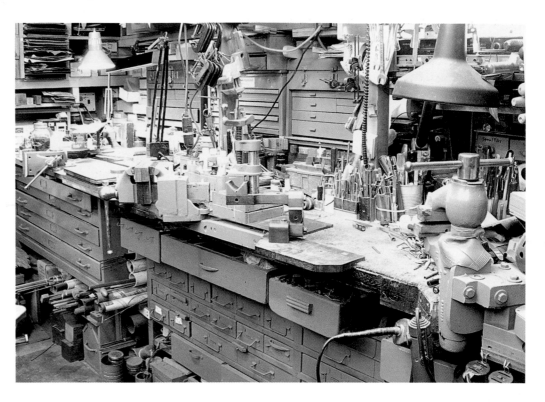

My workbench in 2005 is quite a bit different than the bookcase I started out with.

concentrating on it. For lack of a scientific explanation, I'll call it a learned response. Practice is good!

Knifemaking is a touch and feel kind of thing. Most of what we do with our hands cannot be reduced to formulas and methods. There are some things I do that took many attempts before I mastered the skill or methods necessary to make them work. It's the same way with my inventions. I use an upside-down platen for flattening dagger blades; it took me three years to refine before I finally made it work. The secret of success is to never give up.

The Shop

A large shop is not required to get started. I use the term shop rather loosely because I made my first knives in the closed-in sun-porch of the apartment in which we lived. A shade tree, an apartment in New York City, a lean-to on the back of your house or garage will do. That sun porch wasn't very large but I didn't have a lot of tools either. I didn't have a vise at first, just my homemade grinder mounted on a bookcase and an electric hand drill. I told that so no one will have an excuse that they don't have a place to make knives.

The shop I've been in since 1969 started out as a typical double garage hooked on to our house. It became a real shop in 1975 when I had the double door taken out and a wall put in. I've spent a lot of time to set it up exactly the way it should be and I feel real comfortable in it. I

did the numbers one time and I've spent something like 94,000 hours in my shop since I went full-time in 1973. It's so full of equipment and junk that there isn't room to add anything without a major shuffling of machines. It's my giant comfort zone and I'm always happiest when I'm in there making knives and experimenting with machines and methods.

My smithy is in a lean-to on the back of the shop. The dirt floor has a layer of loose bricks on it that creates a fatigue-free surface. The bricks are laid out with a small gap in them. Loose dirt is swept into the cracks and with use the floor gets a fairly solid feeling. The irregularity keeps the feet and legs moving and that's what eliminates the fatigue experienced on a solid concrete floor.

Setting Up The Shop

Think of it as needing two different areas, one clean and one dirty. The drill press and grinders are the dirty part. The finish bench and leatherwork areas are the clean part. It would be best to have a separate room for grinding and many makers are doing that today. A bladesmith grinds probably 60 percent less steel than a stock-removal maker so the mess isn't as great. I rely pretty heavily on good ventilation and haven't felt the need for a separate grinding room. I keep the dirty operations in the back end of the shop and the clean areas near the front.

You'll be spending part of your life in the shop so

it is wise to set it up to be efficient and safe. A sturdy workbench is the first and most important item. Don't scrimp on wood, 4 by 4 posts for the legs and a heavy top of particleboard or plywood over 2 by 4's. Bolt and glue it together and brace the ends and back with plywood to make it stiff. It should have shelves underneath for boxes or drawers to fill with lots of heavy stuff. That's so the bench doesn't move around when you're filing or sanding on a knife handle.

The workbench I made for *the $50 knife shop* project had three legs with a post vise on the end with one leg. Three legs keep it level on uneven ground but the bench is top-heavy and isn't very stable to work on. It needs about 500 pounds of steel on the bottom shelf for ballast.

A good vise is the first thing to put on the new bench. I mount mine at an angle on a piece of heavy steel that

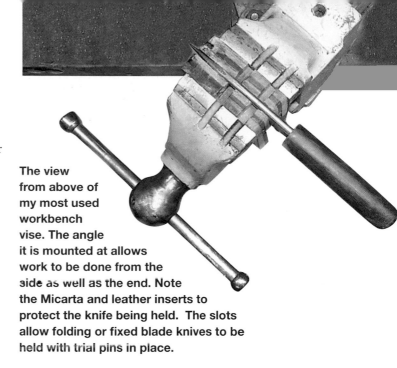

The view from above of my most used workbench vise. The angle it is mounted at allows work to be done from the side as well as the end. Note the Micarta and leather inserts to protect the knife being held. The slots allow folding or fixed blade knives to be held with trial pins in place.

The author as teacher. He is demonstrating his interesting occupation of forging blades and then making them into finished knives.

This is the high-tech area of the Goddard Knife Shop in 2003. The Clausing surface grinder, 1935 Atlas lathe and a no brand name knee mill back in the corner. The indoor forge area is in the foreground, the ball-peen hammer collection on the wall.

My granddaughter Alicia Weaver made her first and only knife in 2001. I'm always amazed at how quick the young folks learn and adapt. Grownups have had too much time to get their own ideas about how things should be done, they are generally harder to teach than kids.

overhangs the bench. This gives clearance to work from either the side or end. If you have room to work at the end of your bench the vise can be mounted square with the bench. It will be more useful if it overhangs the bench by about 8 inches. See the photo.

I use knife boards a lot. A knife board is a piece of wood or Micarta that is cut to the shape of the blade. It supports the blade for drawfiling or hand-sanding. See the picture. The knife board is held in a vise that is mounted so that the jaws are horizontal with the floor. This vise is also mounted at an angle to the bench.

Here are some pictures that will serve as a shop tour. I've been in this garage/shop since 1969, as a full-time maker since 1973. I figured that is about 94,000 hours, which has given me lots of time to get it set up the way I want it.

I tore the inside completely apart and put it back together about 18 years ago. The purpose was to eliminate a large stand-up bench and replace it with a lower bench that was at a height at which I could work while sitting on a shop stool. My knees were both bone-on-bone, however, two total knee replacements in 1996 solved the pain problem. Today I stand up at my sit-down bench probably 50 percent of the time.

In 2002 I tore apart the back end in order to get all the machine tools in one place. The picture will explain itself.

Forge or Grind, Which Will It Be?

The main advantage of forging is that a grinder is not an absolute necessity. The blade can be shaped with a hammer to the place where there is very little metal to remove to finish it. After the blade is annealed it can be completely finished with handwork. However, most forged knives require a fair amount of stock removal once the forging is complete.

The stock-removal method can be done indoors or in a basement where forging would be impractical.

I'd venture a guess that 70 percent of the knives being sold at handmade knife shows have stock-removal blades made of stainless steel. Stainless steel can be forged but it is slow going and in my opinion nothing beneficial is gained. In my opinion the only reasonable way to make knives of stainless is by stock removal.

Others prefer a damascus blade. Most damascus blades are made by forge welding. It is then usually forged from the billet into a bar or blade. If you want to make your own damascus steel you need to be set up for forging. I tell my students the best reason for being a bladesmith is to make damascus steel.

There are many stock-removal makers who purchase damascus bar stock and make knives without forging. Many damascus patterns are available today from those

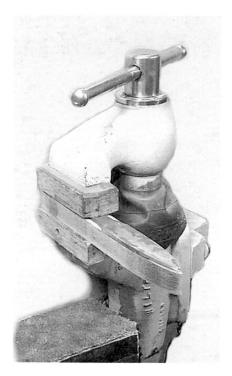

This Wilton is mounted in the horizontal position. I replaced the messed up steel jaws with Micarta and extended them to give clearance. The vise is holding a knife-board with a blade secured against it. The horizontal jaws are handy for holding many things, including a motor tool when carving stag or whatever.

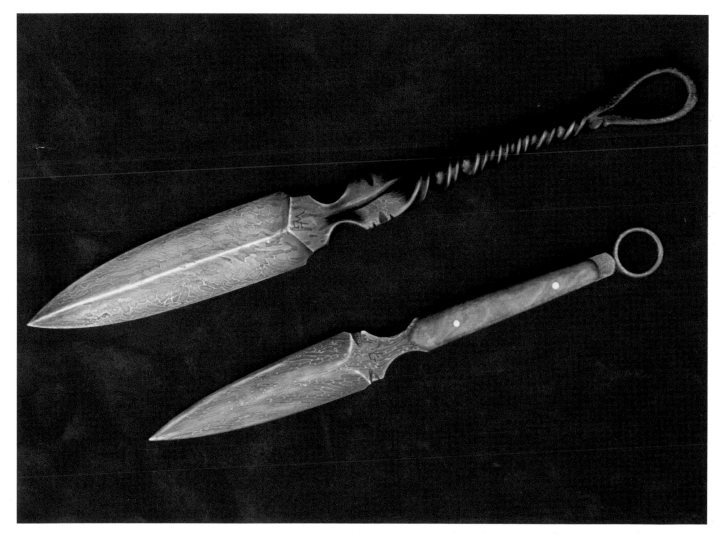

These double-edged knives of damascus steel could only have been made by forging. Forging gives a freedom with the material that the stock removal maker does not have.

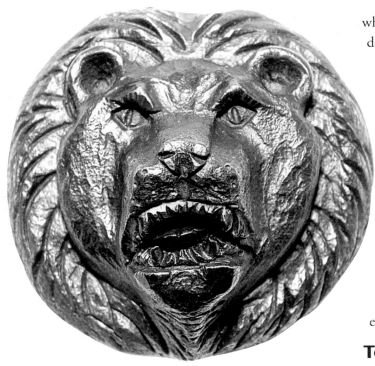

Animal head that was hot forged, chiseled, punched and carved by Daryl Nelson, another artist in hot steel. The material was an axle shaft, which was upset into the 3-inch knob, which was then worked into the animal head.

The frog was forged integral to the 1-1/4-inch steel bar stock by David Thompson who is a true artist in steel.

who make the material to sell. With straight-layered damascus the pattern usually shows up as parallel lines and the blade just does not have the beauty that it would have if it was forged to shape. With the development of particle-metallurgy damascus it is possible to make damascus blades where the only forging was the reduction at the steel mill of a huge billet into blade-sized bar stock or plate.

I've added two pictures that have nothing to do with knifemaking but have everything to do with forging. These two pieces from my collection show several ways that common steel can be hot worked into something artistic.

What will it be for your first knife, stock removal or forged? Think about the advantages of each method and then decide.

Tools Needed For The $50 Knife Shop

It is assumed that you know about garage sales, thrift stores, flea markets and scrap yards. It will be even easier if you are adept at Dumpster diving. If not, you might not be able to set up for both forging and grinding and keep the budget under $50. As I wrote this for the first edition it was Saturday, April 22, 2000 and a fine spring day in Oregon. I visited some garage sales in my neighborhood. I spent $4 on tools and got half a dozen items from the free piles that will be used for future projects. As I work on this new edition it is August 5, 2005 and I just scored big on a $5 box of assorted tools and such. One item was a new $9.95 abrasive cut off wheel, still in the package, and that was just the start.

Bare Essentials, Tool, and Material List

1. Safety glasses or facemask.
2. Homemade grinder, or whatever you have.
3. Hand drill, or electric, with drill bits to match the pin size.
4. Sanding attachment for the electric drill and assorted disks from 60- to 320-grit.
5. File for steel. Optional, a wood rasp for rough shaping handles.
6. Sharpening stone, silicon carbide wet or dry paper will work if you don't have a stone.

Left to right: A simple knife board with a blade in the working position. In the center an "improved" model knife vise made of wood. At the right a heavy-duty knife vise uses wedge power to hold a knife by the blade.

The original $50 Knife Shop. Individual items are described as the lessons progress.

7. Heat source: My first choice is the BernzOmatic® JTH7 propane torch made for the 16 oz bottles. It is superior for use with the one-brick forge. (See the chapter "The World's Smallest Forge." Second choice, a coal forge and blower.

8. One soft, high temperature firebrick and several hard ones are required for the one-brick forge.

9. Blade material: Lawnmower blades, old files, coil springs from automobile front ends.

10. Sandpaper, coarse, medium and fine.

11. Fine steel wool.

12. Magnet (salvaged from a blown speaker) or better yet, the small telescoping type from the nearest dollar store. The magnet is used to check for the correct hardening temperature.

13. Quenchant for heat-treating, one or two gallons of oil will do. It can be cooking oil or fat saved from the kitchen, automatic transmission fluid or hydraulic oil. Mixtures of the above listed things will also work. The quenchant should be in a metal container with a lid so that a flame up can be snuffed out.

14. Toaster oven, thrift-store or yard sale variety.

15. Back-up stick for the sandpaper.

16. Wood for the knife handles and items 15 and 17.

17. Knife board, 2 inches by 3/4 inches by 12 inches and wooden knife vise.

18. One or two C clamps.

19. Wire for pins, (nails, coat hanger, welding wire, whatever)

The following are needed if you are going to forge a blade.

20. Steel chunk or a real anvil. (See the chapter on makeshift anvils.)

21. Rake, poker, shovel, and a water dripper. (A fireplace poker and shovel will work and any tin can will work for a water dripper.)

22. Two metal 5-gallon buckets one for water, one for coal.

23. Tongs or Vise Grip-type pliers.

24. Hammer, 2- to 3-pound cross peen or whatever.

25. Stiff wire brush for scale removal.

In keeping with the low-bucks approach, all materials used in the project to make knives with primitive equipment were either scrap or discarded. Spring steel from a junkyard car was used for the forged blade. A worn out lawnmower blade furnished the steel for the stock-removal blade. I used oak from pallet boards to make the knife board, blade vise, sandpaper back-up stick and handle slabs for the stock-removal knife. A piece of a tree branch was used for the handle material on the forged blade. A steel coat hanger was used for pin material. Thrift store materials were utilized for the forge and junkyard material for the anvil.

The photo shows all the major components of *the $50 knife shop*. I feel good about making beautiful knives out of steel that otherwise would have ended up in a landfill or being melted down to make plowshares or toasters. It takes a lot of our natural resources to make new steel. I like to feel I am helping in some small way by recycling everything possible. For more on this approach to knifemaking see the chapter "Primitive Knifemaking."

CHAPTER 2

THE FORGED KNIFE

Forges

My smithy is in a residential neighborhood and I would have a difficult time trying to work with coal. There are some traditionalists who want to work with coal but as a general rule I don't recommend it. I prefer gas because it is clean and efficient. By efficient I mean that I can forge one or two small blades using the gas forge in the time required to clean out the coal forge from the previous fire, lay a new fire and get it burning good.

This is the urban smithy. It looks like all the iron and steel is covered with rust, and it is. Oregon has a mild climate but is also very moist with rapid temperature changes. I gave up on fighting rust and don't clean anything up unless I'm hauling it somewhere where the public will see it.

A look into the mouth of the basic homemade Dragon Breath forge.

My large propane forge/furnaces are all homemade. At present, all are a horizontal steel tube lined with ceramic fiber that is coated with refractory cement. Take a look at the photo and you'll see that they are quite simple. The burner tube is made of black-iron pipe (do not use galvanized pipe). The only new purchased parts are the insulation, refractory cement, pressure regulator, valves and a propane bottle. I find used acetylene regulators at yard sales and so I've never had to purchase a new one. I always have the used regulators checked out by the local welding supply shop. Any needed repairs are usually very economical.

If you want to build your own gas forge you will find plans for many different versions available on the Internet. Pick one that looks simple, they usually work just as good as a highly complicated one. When possible talk to the person who designed it and see if they do the type of work you will expect from it. Before building a gas forge check with the company that you have your fire insurance with. Also, check on local ordinances that apply to be sure you are legal with your creation.

Alternative Forges

I once made a dirt forge by digging a depression in the ground and then placed a pipe into it for an air supply. See the photo. A small blower furnishes the blast for the charcoal or hardwood fuel. To get more heat, place a cover of firebricks over it to create a heat chamber. Once the bricks get hot the metal will heat much faster and the bonus is a larger work piece can be heated than on the open fire. A pile of dirt on any convenient table will work when prepared as above. I did that one time to show a student that almost anything would work as long as fuel and a blower were present.

Make a box by stacking up firebricks, this way any size forge/furnace can be made. Mount a blower on a pipe and stick it into the chamber. Real charcoal will do for a fuel. Charcoal briquettes can be used but don't work very well because the additives make them pop and spit when a blower is used to speed up the burning. A side-draft tuyère works best for charcoal. A coal type firepot with the air supply coming in through the bottom does not work well with charcoal.

An external look at the Dragon Breath forge.

See the chapter on primitive knifemaking to see a forge made in a washtub.

The Tin-Can Forge

Gene Chapman used a coffee can to make the first tin can forge I ever saw. The heat source is a portable propane torch. My favorite portable propane torch is the BernzOMatic JTH7. It is adjustable over a wide range and is hotter on the high end than many other models.

I've made half a dozen different sizes of the mini-forges in tin cans that were lined with Kaowool® brand ceramic fiber insulating material. The liner in this type mini forge should be coated with a layer of fire clay or furnace cement. The flame is directed into the can through a hole in the side. The goal is to direct the flame so that it rolls around the inside of the liner. As the liner heats up, and the heat radiating from the liner heats the work. The tin-can forge is

The Dirt Forge is shown using charcoal for fuel to burn the grease out of wire rope prior to forge-welding it to make wire damascus. After this picture was taken I stacked fire bricks over the top of the fire chamber and forged a blade using a hay rake tooth for material.

The pipe tuyere is shown as installed in the barbecue. This picture was taken before I drilled more holes in the tuyere. The "L" shaped tool is a rake for managing the coal.

simply a miniature of the tube-type homemade gas forges that many other bladesmiths and myself use.

A Mapp or oxygen/acetylene gas torch can also be used and either type will give more heat than propane. Such torches will make it possible to heat larger pieces than with propane. Steel should not be heated over 2,100 degrees F. Be very careful when using oxygen/acetylene, the 5,600 degrees F flame will destroy anything that gets too close.

A Cheap Coal Forge

The simplest and most economical forge to make is the pipe tuyère coal forge. (Tuyère: French, pronounced to-weer, means "stem of a pipe" or air supply when applied to a forge.) The Hudson Bay Company used this type of forge where they set up supply bases. Railroad blacksmiths have described this type forge as being used in their shops. One advantage is that it can be made any size that is needed.

Making a Pipe Tuyère

The pipe should be a minimum of 2 inches in diameter and long enough to span the top of the forge table or other base. Note the location of the holes, which should be between 1/4 and 3/8 of an inch in diameter. The number of holes will depend on the type of blower and somewhat on the coal. The pipe I used was threaded and had a cap on the end opposite the hair dryer used as a blower. A wooden plug could be used on the back end of an unthreaded pipe. The plug or cap is removed for the occasional cleaning of the tube.

The pipe can be laid on any type of table with suitable insulation between it and the top of the table. Firebricks or dirt mixed with ash will work for insulation, plain dirt might bake into hard clay that could become difficult to maintain.

The Forge Body

The coal forge I constructed in 1988 for the buckskinner knife project had a rusted out charcoal barbecue for the base. All parts were purchased at a local thrift store for a cost of less than $5 and it took about an hour to assemble it. The barbecue that I used had some holes in the rusty bottom. I put a piece of sheet metal over the holes before building an insulating bottom of firebricks with a mixture of dirt and wood ash on top. The tuyère is situated on top of the insulating material and is held in position by packing the dirt/ash mix up onto the sides of it and also over the end portion of the pipe. The cheap forge worked well for the purpose of my experiment with primitive forges. I also used it for several weeks' normal work. The only drawback was the limited size of fire that could be built because of the size of the barbecue.

If an old barbecue is not available a wooden frame can be constructed to make the forge. The same type of tuyère on a table 4 feet square would be adequate for the largest welding fire that a bladesmith might need. The bottom of the forge top is lined with firebrick, a layer of dirt or ash, or a mix of dirt and ash, which insulates the bottom of the pan.

A coal fire that is constantly making coke takes a lot of coal piled up around the border of the fire. To keep the coal contained it is a good idea to construct a rim on the forge that is 3 or 4 inches high.

The Air Supply

I don't necessarily recommend a hair dryer. It just happened that one came along cheap at the time I was doing the buckskinner knife project. One advantage is that the air blast to the tuyère should be adjustable and most hair dryers are so equipped. The main disadvantage of using a hair dryer made out of plastic is it's easy to melt it down. Almost any electric blower could replace the hair dryer. When a "squirrel cage" blower is used placing an adjustable plate over the intake port should regulate it. As the adjustable plate on the intake is moved towards the closed position the motor runs faster because there is less air resistance on the fan blades. This causes the pressure to stay more constant and this is necessary to push the air through the burning mass of coke. A rheostat will not always work because as it slows the blower, pressure drops and there may be insufficient pressure to force the air blast through the burning fuel.

This is what the cross section of a pipe tuyere forge looks like.

This shows the original one-brick forge set up. It was not the best when compared to what I'm using now with the JTH7 torch. See the picture of the Extendo forge.

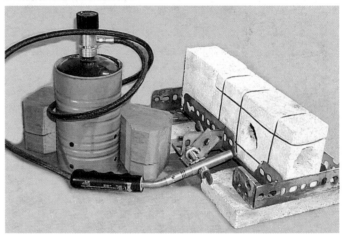

The Extendo Forge, which is far superior to the one-brick model. Note the difference in the propane torches. This is the BernzOmatic JTH7, which is hotter than most torches of this type and yet is adjustable when less heat is needed. Don't settle for anything less.

This photo shows the location of the fire hole in relation to the heat hole.

The World's Smallest Forge

This little forge is not just a novelty item. The one-brick forge makes it possible for anyone who has a small table to set it up on to get started forging.

Mine, (I have several versions); get regular use for forging of blades as long as 7 inches. The one-brick forge is perfect for forging and heat-treating small blades and blades and springs. It is my heat source of choice for forging the rat-tails on my friction folder blades and also the thong holder on the end of a folding knife spring. Probably 70 percent of the work I used to do in the outdoor smithy in my medium sized "Dragon Breath" forge now gets done in the indoor forge area.

Using the side of a carved out brick to heat a section of coil spring for straightening. This is used for work that is too large to fit in the one-brick forge.

The even smaller one brick forge set upright and being used to heat small parts hung on a wire.

The little forge will work with almost any propane torch that will give sufficient heat. However I've found with the BernzOmatic® model JTH7 a wide range of temperatures is available. This torch has a regulator valve at the bottle and a 3-foot flexible hose. This makes it a lot more convenient to set up when compared to the standard torch with the fixed torch head. When forging or hardening small parts, you must be able to regulate the heat to keep the parts from overheating. The JTH7 torch with the regulator built into the valve is perfect for this. The common propane torches without a regulator run at only one temperature, and that is often too hot for small work or not hot enough for large work.

You'll need one soft firebrick for the forge chamber and four or more heavy and hard firebricks as a base. A hard brick won't do for the forge chamber. If you find bricks and don't know what type they are, a weight test will sort them out. A soft, high temperature brick weighs approximately three pounds; the hard bricks seven and a half pounds. As an experiment I drilled a hard brick with a masonry drill, fired up the torch and after five minutes the chamber was not close to glowing. If you don't have any firebricks lying around you will find them in the yellow pages under "Refractories." If you don't find "Refractories", look up a brick mason to find out where they purchase firebricks. The proper nomenclature for the soft bricks is "high-temperature insulating brick". Ask for "New Castle 2,600-degree F insulating brick", or equivalent. Some insulating bricks are suitable for higher temperatures such as 2,800 degrees and 3,000 degrees.

The base for the propane bottle shown in the photo of the original $50 Knife Shop one brick forge is necessary to line up the torch tip with the opening in the brick. The base in the photo is simply a large juice can that is fastened to the wood base with screws. The juice can is a perfect holder for the 16-ounce propane bottle. This base is not necessary if you have the JTH7 with the flex hose. With the JTH7 you might want to build a base of angle iron to hold the bricks and torch holder as I've done with the Extendo forge. This makes a sturdy unit, easy to transport and keeps the half brick in position when using it as an Extendo forge.

There is a difference in the amount of heat that the different types of torch tips put out. The hotter the tip, the quicker the steel will heat up, however many propane torches are too hot for heat-treating. The JTH7 is superior

Dave Rider is up in the woods with his stump anvil and a one-brick forge. He forged a small blade from the tine of an old-time hay rake.

for knife work because it can be adjusted to where it is just perfect to get the hardening heat, and at the high end it's got more than enough heat for forging.

Carve the 1 by 1-1/2-inch diameter heat chamber hole lengthwise completely through the brick with a junk knife blade or drill it out with an old drill bit. The 1-inch hole in the side is named the fire hole; it goes in only far enough to reach the heat hole. The little forge works best and will last longer if the wall of the heat hole is coated with furnace cement. Parker brand "Furnace and Retort Cement" is a 3,000-degree F product that is perfect for coating the heat chamber. I also use it to coat the insides of my large propane forge/furnaces used for welding damascus and forging large knives.

The center of the fire hole should be just below the bottom of the heat hole. This allows the flame to wrap around the work being heated. Gas forges work best when the flame heats the liner and the reflected heat heats the work. If the flame is directed right onto the work it will not get as hot as if it is allowed to wrap around. Don't put the torch tip directly in the heat hole, keep it an inch or so from the opening and aimed so that the flame curls around the heat chamber. Experiment with your torch to see where the flame is aimed to get the most heat. Remember that the torch heats the chamber, the radiant heat, plus the torch flame heats the steel.

After using the mini brick forge for a while the brick started to crack and come apart. I repaired it by wrapping

The English-style anvil with the parts identified.

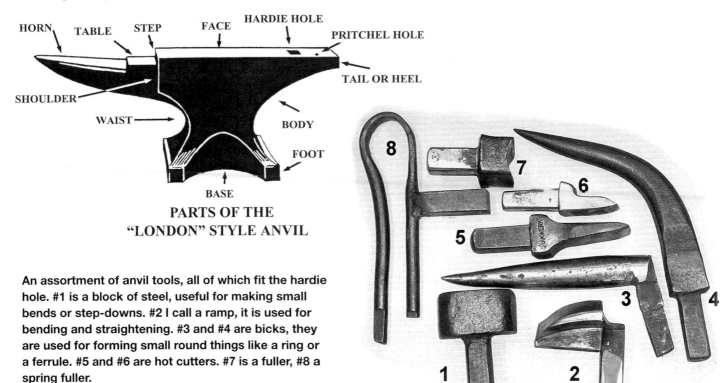

HORN   TABLE   STEP   FACE   HARDIE HOLE   PRITCHEL HOLE

SHOULDER

WAIST → BODY

FOOT

TAIL OR HEEL

BASE

PARTS OF THE "LONDON" STYLE ANVIL

An assortment of anvil tools, all of which fit the hardie hole. #1 is a block of steel, useful for making small bends or step-downs. #2 I call a ramp, it is used for bending and straightening. #3 and #4 are bicks, they are used for forming small round things like a ring or a ferrule. #5 and #6 are hot cutters. #7 is a fuller, #8 a spring fuller.

it with iron wire that is set down in a groove carved in the brick. The photo shows the mini-forge sitting on the hard bricks. When I use it inside my shop it is surrounded on the back and top with hard bricks to support it.

Carve a notch in the side of a soft firebrick to make a cavity large enough for heating parts that are larger than the hole in the mini forge. This works for straightening out coil springs or other curved pieces. The part to be heated is held in the recess where the flame can wrap around it so that it is being heated from all sides.

I've worked up a tempering jig for doing soft-back tempering with the one-brick forge. This jig makes the one-brick forge set-up capable of doing every step in the heat-treating of a blade. See the chapter on heat-treating for a description and picture of the jig.

When using the small forge, I put some bricks at the back of the one-brick forge and then place a heavy brick on top. That's to keep it in place.

I'm getting great reports from those who are using the one-brick forges. One phone conversation was with a maker who was successfully welding small folder-sized damascus billets in a one-brick forge. I can't give him proper credit because the paper-eating monster that lives under my desk ate the sticky-note with his name on it.

He used a "Turbo Torch" from Granger with Mapp gas for fuel. His only complaint was that the borax used for welding flux would eat up the brick. A remedy that may help this is to coat the bottom of the heat chamber with a layer of the furnace cement mentioned above.

Occasionally there is a need to harden small parts and they are best heated and quenched when hung on a wire. This allows the whole part to be quenched at the same time. See the photo for a one-brick forge set up in the vertical position so that the heat comes out at the top. I hang the parts on 1/16-inch stainless TIG wire. Iron wire can be used but it doesn't stand up to the heat as well as stainless. The parts I heat in such a manner include pocketknife springs, small folder blades and lock-bars for locking blade folders.

Dave Rider is having fun with his one-brick forge. Dave is the one who discovered the JTH7 and turned me on to it. He demonstrated with it during "Midnight Madness" at a Northwest Blacksmith Association conference. Those present were very impressed at the amount of work that can be done with it. A short time later he took it camping and set it up with a stump anvil. See the photo. His anvil was a splitting wedge that he reworked. It is driven into the stump and then put to work.

The original $50 Knife Shop Anvil. Now retired and in the collection of Craig Morgan.

The vise on the wood base is called the "Anvil Buddy". He holds hot steel level on the anvil so that the smith has both hands free for hot punching or hot cutting. Anvil Buddy also gives me a place to hang hammers. The anvil is the 150# Peter Wright that is my current favorite when it comes to anvils that have a horn.

is necessary to absorb the blow of the hammer. More weight is needed whenever the anvil and base are bouncing around under the hammer. It's the total that counts; additional weight can be added in the base.

The horn on a traditional blacksmith anvil is rarely used by a bladesmith and ends up being an unnecessary attachment. Some bladesmiths use the horn for drawing-out but it is not efficient for that. The horn is soft, and far from the center of gravity, which make the blows less efficient than they should be. The rounded back edge of the anvil face works much better for drawing because it is near the center of gravity. I wouldn't round off the edge of an anvil with a nice level surface, however, most old anvils are chipped at the edges and rounding it off is a sensible thing to do because it gives you a valuable work surface.

Anvil Advice

Good brands of commercial anvils are Hay-Budden, Trenton, Fisher and Peter Wright. These are usually close to 100 years old and are often worth more to collectors than users. The above listed brands in good condition are worth an average of $2 per pound, new anvils run as high as $5 per pound.

I've bought and sold over a dozen anvils in the last 20 years. My rule is buy cheap and sell high. I currently have a 150# Peter Wright in my indoor forge area with a face that is the best of any I've seen on an anvil that size. The face is very hard and that makes the work a real joy. That's the Peter Wright in the photo with his friend who I named "The Anvil Buddy". This anvil will not be sold, unless I find a better one the same size, and I doubt that I will.

The anvil buddy is a heavy base with an old Parker vise on it. The height is such that bar stock can be held level on the face of the anvil by clamping it in the vise jaws. This is handy for either hot punching or hot cutting when no one is available to hold the stock for you. The anvil buddy is also handy for holding the large bick I made out of the railroad spike-driving hammer. There are times when I am working back and forth between the bick and the face of the Peter Wright.

This type of anvil is a very old thing and is sometimes called a bench anvil. It has a short square tapered section that is driven into a hole in the bench, or a convenient stump.

Dave's material was a spring tooth from an old-time hay-rake, which is simple steel with 1 percent carbon, and that makes it very close to present day file steel. He forged a blade by the light of the Coleman lantern. The JTH burner assembly on his one-brick forge is on the backside and can't be seen. He has it set up to run off of a 20-pound (five gallon size) propane bottle.

The "Extendo Forge" is a recent development that allows the one-brick forge to be extended to make it possible to do longer blades. I've forged and hardened medium weight blades that were not very wide and as long as 10-inches with the Extendo forge. See the photo.

Anvils And Anvil Tools

A good-quality anvil is a specially shaped, heavy chunk of steel with a hard work surface (face). The hard face makes the work easier but is not absolutely essential. Any heavy piece of steel will work and I would say 100 pounds would be is a minimum size to start with. The weight

The value of a hard face on an anvil is not easy to grasp until you have worked on both hard and soft ones. I'd rather work on a small hard one than a big one that is soft. When I first started forging I had a 150# Acme brand cast anvil in my indoor forge area that was about as soft as an anvil could be. I sold it and replaced it with an 85-pound Hay-Budden. The smaller but harder anvil was much easier to forge on. Carry a 3/4-inch or 1-inch ball bearing with you when you go anvil shopping. Drop the ball onto the face from approximately 18 inches. The best anvils will put the ball back into your hand. Any bounce less than 50 percent will make your work much harder.

Anvil Tools

The anvil becomes considerably more useful when a good assortment of anvil tools is available. There are five anvil tools that are essential to the way I forge blades. They include a cut-off hardie, spring fuller, step-down hardie, wedge hardie, and a cutting plate. An anvil tool sits on the anvil and they are usually made to fit the hardie hole. The heated workpiece is usually placed on the anvil tool and struck with a hammer. Occasionally a top-tool will be set on the workpiece and be struck with a hammer. Sometimes an anvil tool will be called bottom-tool because it comes with a top-tool, swages and fullers are in that class. An exception being a cutting plate that can be in the form of a saddle that rides the anvil face. I've got a cutting plate that fits in the hardie hole. Do not use the table on the anvil as a cutting plate because that's not what it's for.

The Makeshift Anvil

I made a makeshift anvil for *The $50 Knife Shop* series. The choice of materials was probably silly; however, it proved my point about using what you have available. All materials were obtained at no cost other than the labor and time to haul them home. The main body is one half of a coupling from a railroad car. I welded it to a base plate, added an upright support and then added steel plates to one side to make a 1-inch square opening for my hardie tools. There is a tapered concave surface on the top where I welded the plates to make the hardie hole. This works great for decorative or other work where a straight bar is bent into a curved section. The weight of the anvil, (135 pounds) plus the heavy particleboard base makes it more than adequate for knife work. Note the spring fuller in the hardie hole.

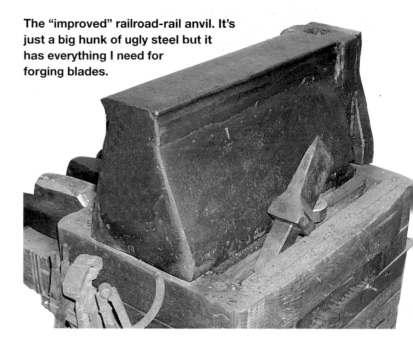

The "improved" railroad-rail anvil. It's just a big hunk of ugly steel but it has everything I need for forging blades.

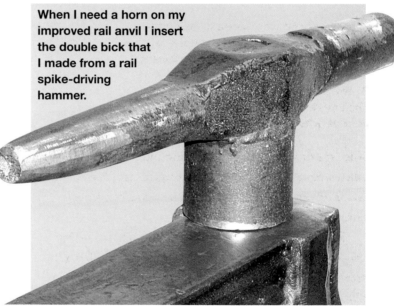

When I need a horn on my improved rail anvil I insert the double bick that I made from a rail spike-driving hammer.

The Railroad Rail Anvil

I spent a lot of time making several anvils out of railroad rail. I got a couple of good anvils but my time could have been better spent doing it a different way. I have the better way started and here is the plan. I turned the rail upside down and cut the base down to a width of 3 1/2 inches and 14 inches long. By using the bottom of the rail I will have a flat surface for my anvil face. I will then torch cut the top of the rail off which will be saved for some future project. The part left for my anvil face will be much easier to harden in it's cut down form. I'll then shape the hardie hole and then heat-treat it and weld it on to some heavy steel to get the weight up to about 125 pounds. It will be much easier to harden the piece of rail

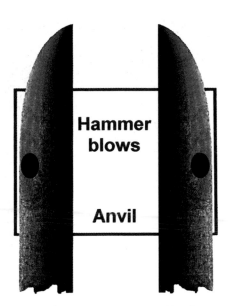

The drawing shows the advantage of having a square or rectangular anvil without a horn. The edge being forged can be placed at the edge of the anvil. That's a Japanese swordmaker's thing. My improved rail anvil is perfect for such forging when I stand at the end opposite the hardie hole.

HAMMER BLOWS

ANVIL

When the blade is in the center of the anvil the hammer overhangs the edge. At the right is shown the clearance for the hammer when using the edge of the anvil.

than the whole piece. The height will be the same as the rail anvil described in the next paragraph, and will sit on the same base.

The anvil I use for most forging at present is made of rail. It was an exceptionally heavy piece, and worn as flat as any I'd ever seen. That means it's somewhat hard from all that use, work-hardened is the correct metallurgical term. I boxed it in with heavy steel and fabricated a 1-inch hardie square hole that is 1 inch from the right end. The top is 3 inches by 15 inches and there is no horn. I made it in two pieces, the main anvil and a sub base, it adds up to about 200 pounds total. It feels the most natural of any anvil I have worked on and I believe it's because I can work either from front end or the normal side position. I think that's the way it is supposed to be… that's why it felt so natural.

When I need a horn I can insert the "bick" made of a railroad spike-driving hammer. See the photo.

In my opinion, the Japanese sword makers had it right all along with their rectangular anvils with no horn. In order to forge right down to the edge of the blade it can't be in the center of the anvil, it needs to be on an edge. That horn thing on blacksmith anvils does not allow the body to be in the correct position to do that. I often find myself working at the front end of my rail anvil.

A Portable Rail Anvil

I put this one together to have an anvil that was easy to haul around. The weight of the piece of rail and the steel between it and the base is about 30 pounds. Added to the steel base and wood column, the total weight is 85 pounds. The total weight isn't bad for forging smaller blades with a 2-pound hammer. (Anvil weight is mostly dependent on the weight of the hammers used.) I used the little rail anvil and the one-brick Extendo forge for three days at a class I taught and got along nicely. I wanted to prove my point once again that a genuine blacksmith anvil isn't necessary for knife work.

The Anvil Base

Any anvil needs to be fastened securely to a heavy base. When the combined weight of the anvil and base is too light if it bounces around from the hammer blows, a heavier base will help the problem. Another solution is to

This makeshift anvil is adequate as a portable unit for light to medium work. The short piece of rail is mounted on some heavier steel to boost the weight. A large bearing race makes a base for the scrap wood support for the anvil and brings the total weight to 85 pounds. Note the cut-off hardie that fits a round hole in the face of the anvil.

put a thick chunk of steel between the anvil and base to boost the weight of the anvil. My favorite anvil bases are made of layers of particleboard, which are glued and nailed together. This type base is heavier than most wood and is always flat on the bottom and level on the top.

The anvil base under my rail anvil described above has enough steel and iron in it to bring the total weight of anvil and base to 485 pounds. This is the most solid anvil I've ever worked on.

The Granite Anvil

Ever since I watched a video of modern African iron makers using a rock for an anvil I've had the craving to see how a rock would work. I started my search for a rock with my friend and fellow knifemaker Carl Sontag. He drives a truck that hauls, among other things, rocks. I asked him to find me a big piece of hard rock for an anvil. He suggested that I contact a monument company to see what they had for scrap. My first call to a monument company was successful. They had a pile of cut-off pieces and obsolete head stones that I could choose from. The best part, it was free for hauling it away. With help from friend John Priest I hauled home a 150-pound granite tombstone and another rectangle of pretty pink granite. The tombstone measures 11 inches by 22 inches by 6-1/2 inches and I'm using it on end for my rock anvil experiment. This stone has the large sides polished and the sides and ends are rough. I chose the best end but it was still pretty irregular.

My first test was to see if it would handle heavy blows. With a piece of cold mild steel on it I hit it dead center on the end as hard as I could with a 10-pound hammer. There was no damage to the granite but it didn't do the steel any good because the rough end of the tombstone was quite irregular with sharp peaks and divots. For safety reasons I deliberately knocked the edges off the square corners. I didn't want a misdirected blow to send granite fragments in the direction of any innocent bystanders.

I had to do some major work to get a good enough surface for my forging experiment. I chipped at it and then ground on it with a 16-grit Norizon® cup wheel on my 2-horsepower Black and Decker "Wildcat" disc grinder. I finally managed to get a flat spot about 1 inch by 2 inches.

The first experiment had the tombstone mounted in the plastic bottom of an old shop vacuum. A mixture of clay and dirt was tamped in to hold it. I went to work forging on a blade on it and managed to do pretty well. Good aim is required to keep the blade on the small flat

I made the base shown for the first new Mankle anvil at the ABS School. The materials were the cut off pieces of 2 by 4 from the test procedures. The only anvil bases there were stumps that were not level. I like to get close to the anvil at times and the rectangular base makes that much easier than a round stump. Plywood or particle-board anvil bases start out level and stay that way, and bugs won't eat them. Mike Sweany is giving the new setup a good test.

The 150# granite anvil.

The granite leather-tooling anvil installed on my leatherwork bench.

space and then hit it where it is supposed to be hit. The forging surface of the anvil took on a metallic appearance by time the blade was finished; it almost had a shine to it. I'll keep working on the striking surface with the grinder in order to get a larger flat. It is a very good anvil, no noise, and solid as a rock. (Pardon the pun.) Bouncing a hammer on the shiny work area indicated a hardness that is close to the best anvils. I've forged two blades on it now and although it is a bit awkward because of the not so flat face, it does serve the purpose of an anvil.

I've made a wood base for the tombstone anvil. At the time I was doing an experiment to see how it worked to forge a blade while sitting down. It worked just fine, except for hot scale falling on my knees. Then, there are always problems to solve with new methods.

A Leather Tooling Anvil

Starrett, maker of precision machinist tools offers pink granite surface plates for layout work in tool rooms and inspection departments. On the ground at the monument company along with the junk tombstones was the cut-off end of a $400 Starrett surface plate. I might not have recognized it but the Starrett nameplate was still on it. I asked about it and it seems a family wanted the surface plate cut down and made into a monument and this was the leftover part. It's the pretty pink rectangle I lugged home with the tombstone mentioned above. It measures 4 inches by 6 inches by 24 inches and at 55 pounds it's just

the right size for a tooling anvil on my leatherwork bench.

Clean And Smooth Forgings

Follow these steps to achieve a forged blade that is both precise and has a fairly good finish. Doing so will make the finishing much easier, whether by hand or with power equipment. It is especially important when using the non-electric method with file, stone and sandpaper.

Uneven hammer blows in forging out the bevels will cause the blade to have an irregular and wavy edge profile. As any protrusions show up at the edge they should be pushed back in with careful hammer work. Keep the edge portion hot and with the back resting on the anvil and as the protrusions are pushed back into the blade remember to keep working at the edge sides to keep it an even thickness. Better yet, forge slow and easy in order to keep from getting the edge profile uneven. If the high spots are left on the edge to be taken off with stock removal the result will be a blade that is thicker at the edge than it should be. The resulting excess amount of steel to be removed from the sides of the blade will make finishing with handwork very difficult and time-consuming. The first blade I finished without electricity went back into the forge two more times before I got it close enough to be finished with file and stone.

The blade must be kept free of fire scale as you go along. When the forge has an excess of oxygen, or if it is running too hot, both will cause an excess amount of scale.

Those are the masterful hands of Don Fogg. Don is using the wet forging technique as he carefully shaped a traditional style Japanese blade. This picture was taken at the Alabama Forge Council Bladesmith Symposium in 1996. Note the old anvil with both horn and tail broken off. It's been said that during the Civil War it was the practice of the troops from the North to break the horn and tail off of anvils found in the South. The damage may have rendered them somewhat inadequate for blacksmithing work but it produces an anvil close to the shape that the Japanese sword makers use.

The big forged knife in the center and the dagger at the bottom were early work in my "Tribal Series."

You will be sorry if you hammer on the blade with scale on it. Each subsequent forging heat can push the scale deep into the surface. Those pits will mean a lot of extra time with the file or grinder to finish the bevels. Such pits will also cause a lot of blades being almost too thin by the time the surface is cleaned up. Use careful and light hammer blows and a minimum amount of heat as you get close to the finished shape.

To help keep scale at a minimum it is important to keep the fire, either coal or gas, slightly rich. A fire with excess oxygen will create a lot of unnecessary scale. A "butcher block" brush has very stiff, flat wires and works very good to scrape the scale off each time the blade is taken out of the fire. Obnoxious scale can be scraped off with the flat end of a planer blade or old file. Keep loose scale wiped off the anvil face because it will be worked into the blade surface if left to contact the hot blade with pressure from hammer blows.

Wet forging is a Japanese method, it's messy but worth the effort. Before each forging heat a Japanese swordmaker will use a mop made of straw to wet the face of the anvil. The hammer is dipped in water to wet the head. When the wet surfaces contact the hot blade it causes the scale to explode and fall off. I've been using this method since 1983 when I saw it in a video of a Japanese sword maker forging a blade. It is an excellent way to combat scale formation on a blade.

Another technique I learned while watching that video was to keep the blade off of the anvil between blows. The swordsmith tapped a rhythm on the anvil with the hot blade and each time the blade touched the anvil the hammer contacted it. This keeps the heat in the blade much longer and is a fun method to practice and finally master.

Forging The Blade

I had been forging blades for about three years when it dawned on me that there was a major advantage of forging that I had never heard of or seen in print. Most of the information advocating the forging of blades had to do with grain refinement, aligning the molecules or something to do with mystical properties that can be achieved by a process known as packing.

My enlightenment came during the time I was working on a tribal series of knives that were based on primitive designs and methods of construction. The simplicity of the construction details taught me that knives could be made with only a forge and a few very simple hand-powered tools. I then did an experiment to finish several knives without any power equipment. The only electricity used was for the hair dryer that served as air supply for the homemade coal forge. The blades were forged very close to shape, annealed, drawfiled, rough finished with hand stones, heat treated and then finished out with hand stones and sandpaper. Carefully forging blades close to the finish shape eliminates the need for a grinder. Burning the tang into a wood handle eliminates the need for any type of drilling machine.

The magazine series started out working with coal. Coal makes a versatile forging fire but I don't recommend it because it's not efficient. When I was half way through writing the *BLADE® Magazine* installments on working with coal I made the first one-brick forge. It worked so efficiently that I used the "World's Smallest Forge" as a heat source for the forged project knife. It will be used for the two projects in this book. The first project in *The $50 Knife Shop* is to make a knife without any power tools, and it will be forged to shape.

Blade Material For The Forged Knife

Perhaps the easiest material to obtain for the project to make a knife without power tools is a coil spring from an automobile front-end. Automobile salvage yards usually have obsolete or broken springs that can be purchased cheap. I once bought 15 pairs of Honda automobile coil-springs for $2 a pair. Most of these are made from a round rod that is approximately one-half-inch diameter. One advantage for the beginner using the spring material is that it takes much less forging to make a small blade from it than if you start with the common size of flat bar which is usually 1/4-inch by 1 inch. The coil spring material is usually 5160 chromium steel or 9260 silicon-manganese steel. The life of a coil spring usually does not hurt it as a material for knives. Don't buy a rusty, bent or broken coil spring, many nice looking springs are out there and are a better choice of material to work with.

Most leaf spring material is also 5160 but is a lot more difficult to work because it is usually too wide to make the average knife. Splitting it with a hot cutter is slow and hard work. An easier solution is to use a cutting torch to split

it into manageable pieces. It is then necessary to get rid of the slag and uneven edges with a grinder. That is one more operation that takes time and time is money. Bargain-priced steel from the scrap yard can quickly become expensive if there is very much labor involved in preparing it to be worked into blades.

An assortment of junkyard steels.

Using the cut-off hardie to cut bar stock.

Using the hot cutter to cut bar stock.

As of August 2005 new 1/4-inch by 1-inch bar stock of 5160 and 1095 are less than $3 per foot when bought by the bar. Admiral Steel in Chicago, Illinois has a wide range of steels for knife makers, everything from carbon to stainless steel and damascus material. Pacific Machinery and Tool Steel in Portland, Oregon is a good source for 5160 and some sizes of 1084 and 1095.

Getting It Hot

You need to get your heat source going; either the mini-propane forge made from a firebrick, the homemade coal forge, or some other heat source. The first step is straightening out enough of the spring to have a manageable piece of material to work with. It is easier if you don't have to deal with the whole spring at one time so If you don't have a cutting torch, find someone with one and have them cut it into pieces that have two complete coils. If you are using the one-brick forge the spring material will need to be short enough to get in the heat chamber. If you don't have a way to get the spring cut into pieces you can do it with heat from the coal forge. Set up a couple of bricks so that they form a 90-degree corner. Place the coil spring right up against the corner in the bricks and hold the torch flame so it can wrap around a section of the coil closest to the brick corner. Depending on the heat that your torch puts out you may be able to get a part of the coil hot enough to straighten and cut off. If you don't have an anvil with a hardie hole and cut off hardie, you'll have to use a hot-cutter or just mush it off on the edge of the anvil. Or you can fast forward to the section on grinders and set up a bench grinder with an abrasive cut-off wheel on it and use that to cut up the spring. The small disc grinders that are so poplar can be set up with an abrasive cut-off wheel. Take the first heat in the center of the spring section and bring it up to a good orange/yellow heat. Quickly pull it apart as far as you can and cut it using one of the methods from the illustration. If you have sufficient heat left after

This is called the mush blow, it uses the edge of the anvil as a bottom tool. It's not the best way to hot-cut bar stock but I've been places where there was no other way. The sharper the edge of the anvil, the better it works.

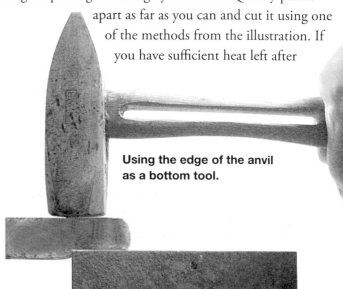

Using the edge of the anvil as a bottom tool.

cutting start the straightening process.

Repeat this process until you have a manageable length of spring stock.

If you are able to get two coils straightened out it will give you a piece of knife material between 20 and 30 inches long. You'll have a built-in handle with no need to use locking pliers or tongs to hold the material while you forge your first blade. This is a real advantage while you are learning because there will usually be misplaced hammer blows that will knock the blade out of the holding device. This is not only frustrating but also dangerous. The time spent working out a long piece of spring material to get a built-in handle is time well spent.

You will need to get an orange/yellow heat on at least 4 to 8 inches of the spring material. Hit the spring with the hammer just hard enough to straighten it out. Flatten the end of the spring material to make it easier to hold with locking pliers or tongs while straightening the other end. As you progress to where approximately one half of the spring section is somewhat straight, grasp the straight end with the locking pliers and straighten the other end. When the material is reasonably straight it is time to start shaping the blade.

Forging To Shape

Forging to shape can be described as hot shaping the blade so that very little stock removal is required. Our exercise to make a knife without power tools will require that we get the blade extremely close to the finished shape by forging it. This is one part of knifemaking that hasn't changed for thousands of years. It may be the low-tech end of blade making but it has one big advantage in the simplicity of tools required. All you'll need is a fire to heat the steel, some muscles to swing a hammer and an anvil where the steel and hammer will get acquainted.

The first smiths laid the foundation for the machine age and that makes forging the beginning of all technology. Forging is not only the most basic metalworking process but a lot of us find it's great fun to heat a piece of steel, take hammer-in-hand and coax the orange-hot steel bar into a new and exciting object.

The 5160 coil spring material used for this project can be forged in the range of 1,600 to 2,200 degrees F. I like to work in the range of 1,800 to 2,000 degrees F. The first step in forging a blade from the round spring stock is to make a flat section is 4-1/2 inches long and 3/16 inch thick. The resulting rectangle will be between 3/4 and 1

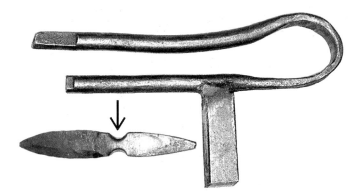

A homemade spring fuller with an example of the work it does.

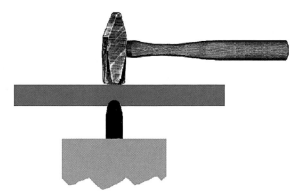

A step down hardie, or hardie swage; it is useful for setting up the area where the blade starts, for either full-tang or narrow-tang styles. It can be used, with care, to start the tang, however the spring fuller is a superior way to do it.

inch wide, depending on how rounded the face of your hammer is. The tang area is then drawn down to 3/8-inch wide with a little taper in it.

To start the tang, hold the point where you want the tang to start over the edge of the anvil. The hammer blow should be directly over edge of the anvil. That creates a step down where the blade meets the tang. By turning the blade 180 degrees the step down on the other side can be forged in with careful hammer blows.

A better way to get the tang started is to use a spring fuller, a tool that you can make for yourself. A spring fuller is easily constructed from any 1/2-inch diameter round bar stock that is at least 24 inches long. Coil spring material or a handle for a bumper jack will hold up better than mild steel. The center section is forged down to about 1/4-inch thick and then heated and bent into the shape shown. While there is still some heat in the bottom part, arc weld a square shank onto it to fit the hardie hole in your anvil. (Arc welding steel with a high carbon content that is not preheated will cause the weld to crack out and fail.) If your anvil does not have a square hole the spring fuller can be held in a heavy vise. A normalizing heat will finish the project and leave the material sufficiently springy.

When reducing the tang portion of a blade to make a narrow tang, never turn it around and around as you hit it with the hammer. It should be reduced in a square or rectangular section till near the right size and then have the corners knocked down to make it somewhat round. If you turn it around and around as you forge it down it can create a pipe or hollow in the center of the steel, that, in turn, will make it weak. This could be a reason for a blade to fail in the tang area.

The Pre-Form

In order to forge a specific blade shape, a pre-form of the blade must first be forged. Each different blade shape has its own unique pre-form. To make the lesson easier to explain I've assigned A to the thickness, B to the width and C to the length of the bar stock. Note dimensions A, B, and C for the steel bar in the illustration.

If a rectangular bar of steel is forged to a point and beveled with no attempt at making a pre-form it will make a wild, crescent-shaped blade that I call a "Buffalo Skinner." This is the blade shape that almost everyone makes for his or her first forged blade. Learning to make the correct pre-form for different blade shapes takes some of the mystery out of forging to shape.

The pre-form is formed in the B dimension with no attempt at forging in the bevels. As the pre-form takes shape the thickness at A will increase. This should be continually worked down with the hammer as it forms. If you get the pre-form correct but the point is fat in the "A" dimension it will be difficult to get the blade shape you want. The excess material, when forged out into the bevel, will make the shape of the point fat and rounded. As you are keeping the "A"

dimension from getting too thick you can actually forge in a slight taper towards the point. This is known as distal taper.

When forging the bevels, the belly of the blade is formed (almost) automatically with very little hammer work on the profile. If the blade gets too much curve or "belly" it can be fixed by pushing the point back down with light bending blows. With practice, the point and blade shape can be forged exactly to shape. When starting out it is allowable to do some stock removal on the profile.

Using A Hot-Cut Pre-Form

Using a hot cutter to shape the pre-form of the point is a quick way to form a blade. And I see no reason not to use it for certain blade shapes. That is the way many old-time smiths did it and probably for good reason. Much of the steel available at the time could not be pointed up in thin sections without coming apart. I found the following in the 1876 book, *American Blacksmithing, Toolsmiths and Steelworkers Manual* by John Gustaf Holstrom and Henry I. Holford. "Never try to forge the point of the knife, but cut it to shape with a chisel." The book does not say why. I believe I discovered the reason for that statement

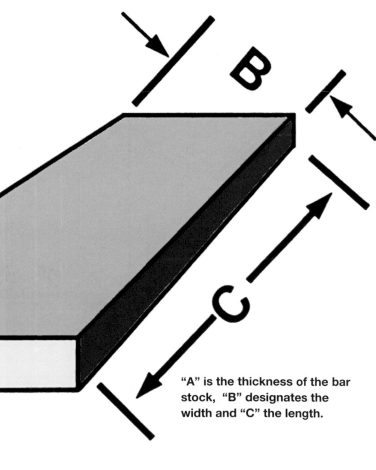

"A" is the thickness of the bar stock, "B" designates the width and "C" the length.

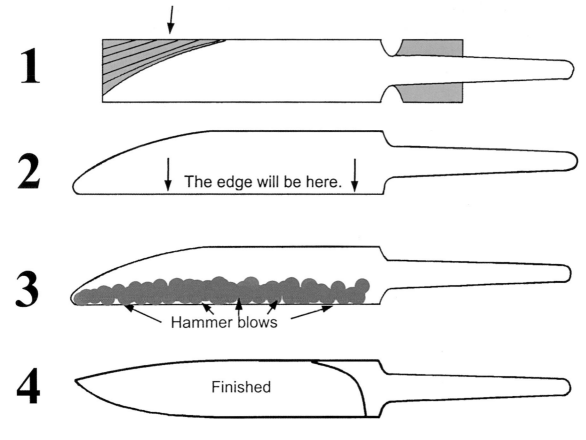

1

2 The edge will be here.

3 Hammer blows

4 Finished

The sequence for forging to shape from a rectangular bar.

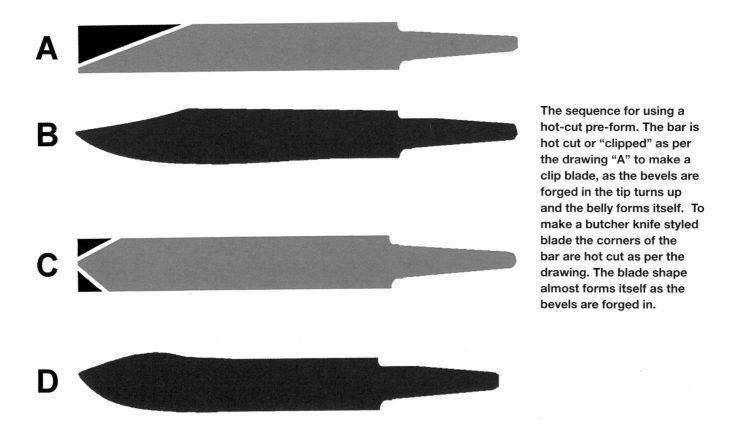

A

B

C

D

The sequence for using a hot-cut pre-form. The bar is hot cut or "clipped" as per the drawing "A" to make a clip blade, as the bevels are forged in the tip turns up and the belly forms itself. To make a butcher knife styled blade the corners of the bar are hot cut as per the drawing. The blade shape almost forms itself as the bevels are forged in.

The wedge hardie, used for either straightening or putting more curve in a blade.

after trying to forge some old cast steel to shape. It split and came apart no matter how I tried. Most steel in the period covered by the author's experience would have been crucible cast steel. Using a hot cut pre-form eliminated the problem of cracking with the steel types of their time.

Be aware that the American Bladesmith Society requires forged-to-shape blades for their standards. Hot cutting a pre-form is not allowed.

The Two Types Of Blows

There are two types of hammer blows that arc used when shaping the blade. The first is the forging blow and the anvil is always directly under the work. A bending blow is made with the anvil surface away from where the blow is struck. The bending blow changes the shape without reducing the size. Many of the kinks and twists that happen in a blade are the result of accidental bending blows. A bending blow is used to push the point of a blade down or put the drop in a full-tang handle. The bending blow is struck just past the centerline of the horn or just off the back edge of the anvil and pushes the end of the part being moved down to the desired position. The wedge hardie is a bottom tool that is useful for getting curve into or out of a blade.

The hammer blow is on center to make a forging blow.

The bevel in the blade is usually forged down to within 20 percent of the finished thickness. When power equipment is used the remaining material is taken off with a grinding wheel or an abrasive belt. For the project to finish a knife without power tools it will be necessary to get it as close as possible to the finished cross section. If not, it will mean a lot more time required with files to work it down prior to heat treatment. After heat treatment it will be all hand stones and sandpaper, one more reason to get it thin in the forging process.

Once the blade shape is nearly finished it is time for some thermal treatments. The last forging heats are actually the start of the heat-treating process. The sequence is as follows: finishing heat, normalizing or thermal cycling and then annealing. Go to the section on heat-treating for an explanation of these processes.

A Final Check Of Straightness

Kinks, twists and bends are hard to see while the blade is hot. The following is the procedure I use to get them ready for heat treatment.

Once the blade has cooled after the annealing process it should be cleaned up by drawfiling or with a grinder to

The hammer blow is just off center in order to bend the tang down.

its finished profile. This allows a better look at how straight the blade is and it is easily checked for twists, kinks, or whatever. The blade is first checked with a straight edge for bends. I check the blade and tang separately and straighten them as necessary. Once I am satisfied with the two ends I make sure the blade is in line with the tang. I do my normal straightening at room temperature by using a three-point setup in a vise.

Twists are harder to spot so I lay the blade on a flat piece of steel for a visual check. Then I will touch first the tip, then the butt portion to see if it rocks.

I will then grind the blade to a little higher degree of finish. Many times I will find problems that the visual check did not find. I'll give it another normalizing treatment when I have to do a lot of straightening or grinding to get a blade evened up.

The Final Grind Prior To Heat-Treating

The profile was finished earlier but this is where the bevel is worked down to about 80 percent of the final thickness. Blades that are ground too thin at this point will often warp or even crack when quenched. There should be no deep scratches around the profile. These can act as stress risers and start a crack. I like to have the grinding marks running lengthwise on the outline of a knife. This can be done by hand with fine stones or sandpaper, or with a fine-grit abrasive belt if a belt grinder is available.

Working With Coal

Even though I don't recommend working with coal I've included the instructions here for those who want to do so. And, it was part of the original *BLADE® Magazine* series, *The $50 Knife Shop*.

Good quality smithing coal is the best investment you can make once you decide to use it for fuel. You won't be able to truly appreciate first-class coal until you've had to work with the bad variety. Blacksmith coal may be found by searching the yellow pages under Farrier or Blacksmith supplies. If you don't find a supplier, call a farrier or blacksmith and ask them where they get their coal. However, many blacksmiths now use their coal forges as tables to set propane forges on.

In 1991 when I taught at the ABS School in Arkansas the coal was so bad it wouldn't even make coke. It put out more volume of different colors of hazardous smoke and fumes than I had ever seen. It made my instruction

and the learning for the students very difficult. I told the management that I wouldn't be back unless they got some gas forges. The last two classes I taught went much better with almost enough gas forges to go around. The students got a lot more learning done by not having to waste time with their coal fires. I taught three of the two-week basic bladesmithing classes there and only had two or three students that planned to work with coal.

The First Fire

Make sure that all the lumps in the coal are broken up into pieces no larger than a walnut. Most coal will make better coke if it has soaked in water for some time, but you may as well go to work whenever it is broken up and wet. Don't worry about the fine dust and little particles; they will all stick together in the coke-making process.

The purpose of the first fire is to make enough coke in order to get the second fire going. The first fire is usually not suitable for forging a blade. Coal is full of impurities and does not burn clean and hot if it's not put through the coke-making process. Coke is the byproduct of burning (cooking) coal to get the impurities out.

To lay (start) your fire put an empty three-pound coffee can on end over the air holes in the homemade pipe tuyère. Dump enough of the damp, broken-up coal into the forge to give a depth of 3 to 4 inches and pack it down tight around the coffee can. Remove the coffee can so that you can build a fire in the cavity.

"Now, that's an ugly fire!"

Some coal will start burning with the heat from several sheets of waded up newspaper. Other coal will need a fire made with small wood scraps. Until you figure out the best way for your coal, do it this way: Take four full sheets of newspaper and wad them up one over another into a ball. After lighting the ball of paper, place it over the air holes in the tuyère. Add some small kindling and when the kindling is burning well add a little air from the blower, not too much or you will blow the fire out. Add some small chunk-wood and increase the blast. As the wood starts burning use the rake to work loose coal up onto the

sides of the fire and increase the blast. Always keep a small opening in the center for the flame to come out. The flame will burn the smoke being emitted and that will cut down the polluting of your neighborhood. Common sense must be used here as to how much coal to add and how much air to put into the fire. All fires are different because of the variances in coal. You'll have to practice with a coal fire to get good at it.

Keep adding coal by raking it onto the fire or adding it with the shovel until there is a burning mound of coal 8 to 10 inches deep over the tuyère pipe. Pack the coal up onto

Here is Phil Keeley using his patio as a smithy. It's a simple setup but all that he needs. I too worked on my patio before I built a lean-to along the back of my house. The point is to get started with whatever space you have.

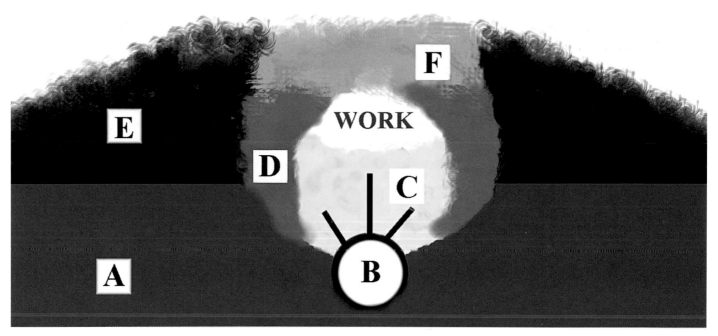

This shows the cross section of the pipe tuyere (B) with the coal fire in progress. (A) is the dirt and broken brick insulating layer in the bottom of the forge. (D) shows the zone where coal is being converted to coke. (E) is unburned coal. The lines show the air flow through the burning coke, (C) and (F) indicates a layer of coke that holds the heat in the area where the work is heated.

the sides of the burning coal with the rake or shovel. Let it burn for five minutes or so and then turn the fire over with the shovel and let it burn for another five minutes. At this point use your instinct and common sense to know how much cooking is necessary to make coke. If you run the blast too long the coke will be burned up. If the blast is not run long enough the coke-making process will not be completed. When you think it has burned long enough, turn off the air and sprinkle the fire lightly with water and allow it to burn out. I remove the blower from the pipe after turning off the air so that the heat buildup does not damage it. Flammable gasses can back up into the blower and start burning. It's not good to go off and leave a coke-making fire until it's totally out. It's good to check the fire occasionally to make sure it does not flame up and burn itself up. If the coal wants to keep burning just sprinkle more water on it.

In an hour or so, or whenever the fire cools down, rake the unburned coal away from the coke, pick out the coke and put it in a separate container. The coke will have a gray crystalline appearance compared to the black color of the coal. If everything went well there should be enough coke to forge the knife blade. When all the good coke and unburned coal have been picked out there will be a layer of ash, clinker and very small coal particles in the bottom of the forge. Scoop this out and discard it.

These instructions are for average coal. Some coal will make coke well enough so that the first fire can be used for forging a blade. You'll just have to figure this out as you progress. The second, forging fire is started with coke and if the coal is good you will always be making enough coke to keep ahead of the demand. Some coke will start burning with kerosene poured on it. Coke from other coal may need a fire started with paper and/or wood scraps.

The most unpleasant part of working with coal is cleaning out the forge prior to building a fresh fire. Unburned coal is returned to the coal bucket. Coke is picked out and put in a separate container. Ash and clinker can be brushed onto the fire shovel and discarded.

The Forging Fire

The forging fire is started just like the first coke-making fire except coke instead of coal is put onto the burning wood or paper. The packed coal will be transformed to coke during the forging process. Add a little coke at a time until it is burning clean and hot. I prefer to build my blade-making coal fire by banking green coal up on the sides to create a trough that is about five inches wide. I then put two or three firebricks over the top to create a furnace effect. This gives more heat with less coke being burned. The fire is maintained by feeding coke as it is needed into the opening at the front. This type of fire will do a lot of work and not burn an excess amount of fuel.

With some coal it is possible to pile a lot of it on top of the burning coke and let it burn until a crust is formed over the fire. A poker is used to make a hole in the front to insert the material to be heated. This type fire is most often used for forge welding. It is maintained by feeding coke into the opening at the front. As the crusty-shell burns out it can be caved in to furnish coke for another covered welding fire or perhaps an open-type fire.

Working with coal will keep you busy. The fire needs constant attention to keep the atmosphere correct. The coke fire is capable of melting steel so the material being heated needs to be watched all the time. The proper forging fire will have a 3- to 4-inch deep bed of burning coke under the material being heated. As the fire burns down, the poker is used to break up the newly formed coke so that it can be worked to the center of the fire. Add green coal to the outer edge of the fire and use the water dripper to keep the coal in the transformation zone from burning up. Keep a good supply of coal banked up onto the sides of the burning coke. As mentioned earlier, keep the center of the fire open with flame coming out and there will be much less smoke.

A coal fire can be divided into four zones. Take a look at the drawing. "A" shows the insulating material in the bottom of the forge. "B" is the air supply, "C" is burning coke, "D" is coal that is being transformed into coke by the heat of the burning coke and "E" is unburned or "green" coal. "F" is unburned coke. The area marked "work" is where you want to keep the blade material. It is on top of the burning coke, not stuck down into it. The "deep" fire allows most if not all of the oxygen introduced by the blower to be burned before it reaches the work piece. The fire is called "shallow" when it is allowed to burn down close to the air supply. This is not good because there is not only less heat but there will be an excess amount of scale formed on the steel because the oxygen has not been consumed at that part of the fire.

Every so often the poker should be used to clear any clinkers that have formed over the air holes in the pipe tuyère. Small clinkers can be pushed away from the air supply; the larger ones can usually be hooked with the end of the poker and pulled out. With good coal you may be able to work several hours without having to turn off the blower and clean out the ash and clinker.

It takes time and patience to learn to properly maintain an efficient coal fire but I think it is worth it. Coal fires are more versatile than a gas forge. This is good for the blacksmith but not as important to the bladesmith.

If I lived in the country and didn't have to make my living making knives I would probably burn coal for some of my forging. The only true disadvantage other than the smoke and dirt is in production time. There is always the time involved for the clean-out party before the next forging session and it takes time to get the coal fire started. With gas I will have two or more blades forged by the time I have a coal fire ready for the steel.

I like making the knives out of wire rope that have a loop of cable for the handle. It's easier with coal to get a localized welding heat on the blade portion when welding the two ends together that make the blade. With a gas forge it is impossible to get the type of localized heat possible with coal.

The all-steel knives shown in the photo are forge welded of wire rope. They are best done in a coal fire because a localized welding heat is possible. Welding this style knife in a gas forge is difficult; I've even gotten the tongs welded to the handle when getting the blade portion welded up.

CHAPTER 3

THE STOCK-REMOVAL METHOD AND FINISHING

Making knives by the stock-removal method is easy. Simply take a bar of steel and grind away everything that doesn't look like a knife. That's an old joke, but there is a lot of truth in it. A rectangle of steel is picked out that is wide enough to make the design and of a proper thickness. The first step is sawing or grinding the finished profile of the knife. This is the easy part because very little coordination is required. The fun starts when the bevels are ground into the blade. A belt grinder is the easiest way to create the flat wedge that makes a blade what it is. Assuming the platen is flat, the wedge will be fairly flat. Using a grinding wheel creates a challenge in finishing because all those little grooves from the wheel have to be smoothed out. See the drawing.

The faithful reproduction of my first grinder from 1963.

There are very few modern makers who don't use a belt grinder, but I want to stress the point that making a knife can be done without such a tool. James Black, William Scagel and all those old-time makers did it without belt grinders. In fact it was a century after the height of the bowie knife era when the belt sander was first made in the 1930s.

I made my first several hundred knives with only a grinding wheel and a disk sander. (My excuse is that I didn't know any better.) It's not a way I would recommend to be competitive with the best of what is being done. I do recommend it for those who want to make some simple hard-working knives with a minimum of investment in equipment.

My First Knife

The year was 1957 and I was in my senior year of high school. I got the inspiration to make knives when I watched my wood-shop teacher cut up Japanese sword blades and make hunting knives out of them.

I found a couple of worn out beet topping knives at a second-hand store. I marked out the shape of butcher knives with chalk and had the Agriculture Shop teacher torch cut them out about a half-inch oversize. I ground on those blades with a bench grinder for what seemed like days. I was overly concerned about getting them hot enough to spoil the temper. I was so carefully grinding I doubt those blades ever got over 100 degrees. Once they were rough ground the blades were smoothed up with a disk sander designed for woodworking. I used copper harness rivets to attach handles made from an old desktop. I sold one of them to my teacher, two more to a neighbor and have no idea what happened to the others. I've never counted those as a starting point for my career because they were not made from raw steel.

It was 1963 and I built a makeshift grinder out of a washing machine motor. I then made my first knife from scratch. It was ground out of a lathe rasp because it was the only material I had. The choice of material was good because it did not need to be hardened. The carbon content was high enough to make an excellent cutting blade. Tempering in the kitchen oven at 375 degrees F was all that was required. (An old blacksmith told me the temperature to use.)

The only drawback with the lathe rasp was the thickness. My grinder was not very efficient and I didn't know what I was doing so it was slow going. I could have

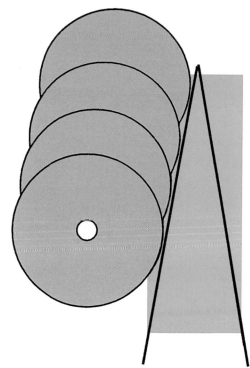

This shows the action of the tracks made with the grinding wheel to shape the wedge that makes a blade cross section.

This is what a beet toping knife looks like. I had a new one for the picture in the first edition. Recently I found an old, beat up one that is more like the ones I found in a second hand store in Gooding, Idaho. The authentic beat up knife came from a trading post in Caldwell, Idaho. I found it while on my tool search for an upcoming project, The $10 Knife Shop.

made a blade out of thinner material in much less time and I would have had a better knife. The finished blade was thick and clumsy but worked well enough to field dress a couple of bucks I shot with a muzzleloader. Back then I didn't have enough experienced to know when a blade was too thick, I believed heavy was good.

That knife was for sale the first year I was making and selling knives and it's only by pure luck I have it. Everyone wanted the "improved" workmanship of the subsequent models. By the end of that first year I decided it would

The two knives span the 42 years of Goddard knives. The knife on the left is the one that got me started on my life's work back in 1963. The one on the right is from 2005 and was ground and disc-sanded smooth using the Good News Grinder. It was my working knife project for the Krause book, BLADE's Guide to Making Knives.

be a good one to keep. I'm glad to have it because it helps me prove some points with new or want-to-be makers. It shows that a knife can be made with a $5 grinder and an electric drill. It clearly shows that I didn't have any natural-born talent for knifemaking. I believe the main requirement is a strong desire to do it and years of hard work and practice will get a maker a lot closer to success than any talent they may have at the start.

As time went by the working knives I make got thinner, lighter and simpler in construction details. With that in mind I cooked up a thin-bladed stock-removal project for the Good News grinder. See the section on homemade grinders.

I chose a lawn mower blade for material to make

the stock-removal knife for several good reasons. 1) The rectangular shape made it easy to cut out the blade blanks with the abrasive cut-off wheel. 2) The material was not too thick, which means less time grinding it to shape. 3) I just happened to have a newly acquired blade from a recently deceased Black and Decker electric mower.

Other potential sources of steel that will make good knives are saws, files, coil and leaf springs. If you have a source of steel that you are unsure of, skip ahead to the materials section and read the chapter on detective work.

The Good News Grinder

The photo shows the Good News grinder fitted with a work rest made of scrap wood and set up and in use as an abrasive cut off machine. The work rest is essential for accurate profiling of a blade and for safety when using the grinder as an abrasive cut-off saw. The work rest should be constructed so that the work surface is just under the centerline of the wheel. It is held in position with a 3/8-inch bolt secured by the wing nut visible between the wheel and motor. The table of the work rest is slotted so it can be removed without having to take the bolt out. The adjustment also makes it simple to keep the table adjusted close to the wheel. If a gap is left between the work rest and the revolving wheel the force can wedge a finger or thumb against the wheel. When an abrasive wheel traveling at a speed of 60 plus mph meets flesh, the wheel usually wins the race.

Leather gloves and a face shield or safety goggles should be worn when using grinding wheels and abrasive cut-off wheels. Wear a heavy apron or an old heavyweight cotton shirt as protection against flying sparks. The cut-off wheels used should be the type with a fiberglass-reinforced web built into them. They are extremely tough but can be broken if the work being cut is not pushed straight into the wheel and supported by a work rest. Eye protection should be worn 100 percent of the time in the shop. I recommend both a full-length facemask and safety glasses whenever using grinding wheels. Safety glasses will only slow down a large piece of broken grinding wheel where the modern face-shields are designed to stop the flying pieces.

An abrasive cut-off wheel was placed on the grinder and the lawnmower blade was sliced into five pieces. This type of cut-off wheel is available at most industrial or welding supply stores. The one I used started out on my 14-inch chop saw. When they wear down to 10 inches and 8 inches, respectively, they are put on smaller machines.

The Good News Grinder making sparks.

The Good News Grinder as an abrasive cut-off machine.

The largest piece, "E", was used for the stock-removal project knife, which will be a full-tang with an overall length of 8-1/4 inches, the handle will be 4-1/16 inches, and the width is 7/8 inches. The blade will be a drop point, the handle straight and in line with the blade. This is as simple a knife as there is. It's sort of a small Green River style knife.

You may prefer to make a narrow-tang blade or perhaps a longer, wider one. Cut the lawnmower blade or whatever material you choose according to the size blade you prefer. Use a scriber or other sharp object and mark the outline of the blade you want to make on the steel.

Profiling the Blade

The abrasive cut-of wheel is taken off and a grinding wheel is mounted on the arbor. A grit size of 40 to 60 is good for rough grinding. It's a shame to purchase new wheels when so many are discarded by saw sharpening shops and saw manufacturers. Check for these sources before purchasing a new wheel.

When I'm grinding the profile I use a push tool to force the steel into the wheel. These are made out an old screwdriver or it would work to drive a large nail into a piece of wood. A slot is filed or cut through the center of the squared off end. This slot rests on the top edge of the

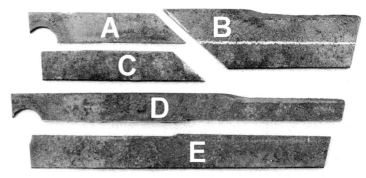

Cut up lawnmower blade.

The lawnmower blade has been cut into blade-sized pieces.

blade and keeps the push tool from slipping off as pressure is applied. Don't bog down the grinding wheel; keep only enough pressure on the blade to remove metal. Little bites taken with the corner of the wheel will speed things up when the grinder is not strong enough to take a full-width cut. The speed of the grinding wheel does the work; too much pressure only slows it down.

Grinding the Bevels

Profiling the blade was the easy part, now the fun starts. Grinding the bevels is the process of removing steel to make a wedge out of a rectangular cross section. See the illustration at the front of this chapter. It shows the action

The Good News Grinder as a sanding machine.

The original $50 Knife Shop sanding machine.

of a grinding wheel to create the wedge shape of a knife blade. The wheel makes a series of bites or grooves that have to be smoothed out with a disk sander, file, or hand stone. See the chapter that follows, "Grinding Advice."

A rotary wheel dresser is a good thing to have when working with grinding wheels. The wheel will load up at times, or get dull; use of a wheel dresser helps keep the rim flat and the wheel removing steel like it should. You might get lucky and find a "star" type dresser in your neighborhood hardware store. If not, then check your local yellow pages for "Abrasives," these folks should be able to tell you a current source for a rotary wheel dresser. If you do not find a local source, go on the Internet and search for MSC, (Manhattan Supply Corporation), they have just about everything.

Smoothing Up the Bevels

I used a disk sanding attachment on an electric drill to smooth the unevenness left from the grinding wheel. See the photo. The knife is clamped to what I call a knife holder. I used coarse and then medium disks. The drill in the photos is a garage sale special. It's a 1950s model Black and Decker that is exactly like the one I used in 1963 to smooth the grinding marks out of my first blade. I did a real nice hand-rubbed finish on the blade made of lawnmower blade steel. See the next chapter for instructions for hand-rubbing a blade.

I recently found a chuck that fits the shaft of the Good News grinder. With a disc sanding attachment placed in the chuck it served as a disc grinder for the project knife for the book *BLADE*'s *Guide to Making Knives*. See the photo.

Grinding Advice

After 42 years it is less frustrating but still not easy for me to grind good blades. Repetition does help build skill but for me it also takes a great amount of concentration. With my own two hands I will stick a blade against the belt and grind where I didn't want to remove anything. You will probably do it too, and all I can say is, "Just don't do it."

Methods, tips and techniques can be learned from a video or watching someone with great skill grind blades. Unfortunately, the time spent will not give you any practice. Spending time grinding 20 blades using good methods will do more to develop skill at grinding than watching a video or DVD twenty times. I have never had a student that showed any talent for grinding blades. Skill always came with practice. Accurate blade grinding requires that the eye and hand be able to make corrections between the blade and belt or wheel that amount to a fraction of a degree. I believe only by repetition can the human body be trained to such a high degree of skill. I don't think it is any different than it would be learning to play a violin.

New makers often will have me comment on their blades. I sometimes hear excuses made because they do not have a better grinder. The machine has never appeared to be the problem. The errors in grinding technique always were caused by a lack of skill or inattention to detail. Thinking back to my reference to the violin, a good one is capable of making beautiful sounds, but only if played with great skill.

Tips for Flat and Hollow Grinding

Some things cannot be reduced to a formula, but following a proven sequence will help with the learning curve. My knifemaker friend Bob Lum is a master at the hollow grind so I had him help me with the hollow grinding advice.

Experiment with the height of the grinder so that you can work without neck and arm strain.

If you have been standing up to grind, try sitting on a stool, this works out good for some makers.

Scale will dull a fresh belt in a hurry. Remove all scale from the sides of the bar stock with a dull belt.

Steel is not necessarily flat and straight when it is received from the supplier. Check and straighten the blade-length stock as needed.

Use a center-finder to lay out two lines on the edge portion of the blade. These usually are spaced out approximately 1/32 to 1/16 inch, a good thickness for the

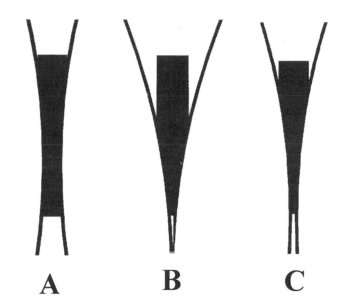

Hollow grinding can leave a blade too thick at the edge as in figure A, or too thick as in B, C is just right depending on the purpose of the knife.

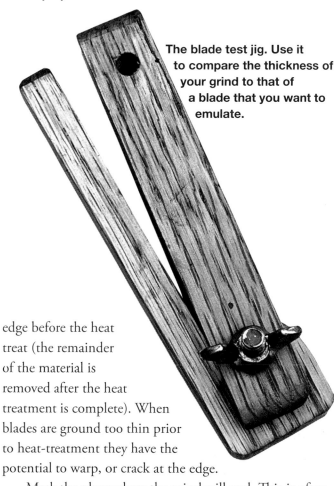

The blade test jig. Use it to compare the thickness of your grind to that of a blade that you want to emulate.

edge before the heat treat (the remainder of the material is removed after the heat treatment is complete). When blades are ground too thin prior to heat-treatment they have the potential to warp, or crack at the edge.

Mark the place where the grind will end. This is often called the termination point or plunge.

Design the blade around the wheel diameter. A wide blade requires a larger-diameter wheel than a narrow blade. If a maker of hunting knives were to have only one contact wheel, it should be a 10-inch diameter.

It's best to grind with the edge up. I remember a phone call from a young maker who called and said he needed help with his grinding. I invited him to my shop for a grinding demonstration. I picked up a piece of steel and started putting bevels on it. He was surprised that I was grinding with the edge up. He had assumed that it was done the other way. His main problem with grinding was that he couldn't see what he was doing. With a little practice he was getting a lot better with his grinds.

The first grind is done at a 45-degree angle. It is used to establish the termination point and gives a witness line at the edge to grind up to. You should leave a flat of at least 1/16-inch at the edge. It is best to use a half-dull belt because it will take so much life off a new, sharp one.

Beginners have the tendency to "poke and look"; the blade is stuck up against the wheel or platen and then pulled back and looked at. This creates a problem with getting a nice even track started. Make a habit of starting a light cut and go the full length on the blade without looking at it. This trains the hand-eye connection faster than the poke-and-look method.

Start the hollow grind with a fresh 60-grit belt. The most common mistake made by the beginner is trying to work with dull belts. Dull belts require an excessive amount of pressure and that means a loss of control. Dull belts heat up the surface of the blade, which can cause irregularities when flat grinding on a platen. Crisp, distinct grind lines and flat and true surfaces require sharp belts. I figure at least three new belts for each knife I make: one for each grit size in the sequence. The finished surface will have to be set up with a sharp belt. Many makers round over the edge of the platen or contact wheel. Carefully break down the edge of the rouging belt with a piece of carbide or old grinding wheel. This will allow a smoother transition between the grind and the ricasso area.

Set the grinder up with good lighting. What works best for me is to have a light on each side of the wheel or platen.

Belt speed will have an effect on control. High speed for a belt is in the neighborhood of 5,000 sfm (surface feet per minute). High speed is good for metal removal but not for control. Some makers, including me, prefer a medium speed of around 3,500 sfm, and I believe the beginner will be better off in this range. My advice is to save the high speed for when control of the blade against the belt has been mastered.

Start the grind at the termination point and be careful not to dip into the blade. A phenomenon happens on blades known as the 2-inch divot. This is where a visible low spot the width of the contact wheel is left in the finished blade. Being careful as the grinding progresses can eliminate the creation of the low spot. To check for this, look at the blade from a low angle with the point towards you.

The position of the hollow grind on the blade will affect the way a blade cuts. A thick blade requires placing the grind higher on the blade. This means a larger diameter contact wheel is necessary. The wheel diameter is a limiting factor, but it is usually better to grind high up onto the blade in order to create a cross section with good slicing ability.

Getting the grinds even on both sides of the blade is a matter of control and practice is the only way I know to achieve it. I have good belt grinders and 42 years experience, but those factors do not keep me from losing my concentration and sticking a blade up against the belt where I should not have. The only thing I can say is; "Just don't do it!"

When I was a kid I took piano lessons for a while. My teacher was always telling me that practice didn't make perfect, perfect practice makes perfect. She was certainly right about that. Practice your knifemaking, and then practice some more. Don't make a hundred knives where the last one is no better than the first. Strive to make each one better than the previous. Some say that a perfect knife cannot be made. I disagree because I'm deluded enough to think I've made at least two that were perfect.

Grind For Good Cutting Ability

Getting the grinds even and smooth is not enough. In order for a blade to have good cutting ability it should have good cross section geometry. The type of material and hardness of the blade and whether it was selectively hardened and tempered will have a lot to do with the degree of thinness that is practical in a blade. A knife blade needs to be thin enough to cut well yet thick enough to have adequate strength for normal use. It is something that has to be worked out with the type of steel and intended purpose of the knives you make. The best way to determine what is correct is to do some actual cutting with the knives you make.

See the drawing of a jig that I made for making a comparison between the cross section of different blades.

The screw is loosened, the first blade inserted, the legs are aligned with the sides of the blade and the screw tightened. Without loosening the screw, the second blade is put into the jig and a comparison is made.

Blade Finishing

Japanese sword blades of the highest quality exhibit perfection in finish and it's all done by hand using natural stones and abrasives. It has always amazed me that such a high degree of blade finishing was accomplished without the use of belt grinders and buffing wheels. The high degree of finish allowed the swordsmith to see if his blade was free of visible defects and the purchaser to ascertain the quality of the blade. It was only natural that a high polish became one of the characteristics of a quality blade.

Hand finishing, when well done, results in a crisp and clean definition of the surfaces that gives a more true appearance than a mirror-finish does. The reflections from the surface of a buffed and mirror-finished blade can cause a visible distortion of the lines and the actual surfaces are not usually as flat and true.

Drawfiling

When doing it all by hand, drawfiling is necessary to establish the final cross section of the blade prior to heat treatment. Draw filing is accomplished by holding the file at each end and alternately pushing and pulling it across the work at 90 degrees to the width. The action on a blade would be to draw it the length of the blade. Draw filing is best done with a standard mill bastard file. A double-cut file will remove material more quickly but will leave small ridges that have to be worked out with the mill bastard file. Draw filing, properly done, leaves a very flat and smooth finish. Some draw filers like to use chalk to lubricate the file teeth, it's supposed to keep the file from clogging. I've tried it both ways and don't see much difference. Once the draw filing is complete the blade is ready to be worked with stones.

Good quality files along with the knowledge of their proper use is a valuable resource for the knifemaker working without power tools. I draw filed the blade bevels on the forged blade for *the $50 Knife Shop* series down to the final shape.

Drawfiling.

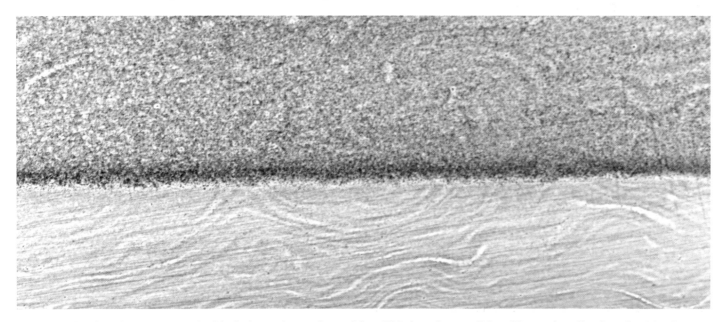

An example of grain structure of a blade brought out by etching. This is only possible with an ultra-fine hand-rubbed finish. The material is from an old saw blade that is probably made of shear steel. Note the distinct temper line from an edge quench.

Hand-Finishing With Natural Stones

The stock-removal, edged-tool makers of the Stone Age had only natural stones for their finish work. The "grinder" of choice would have been the nearest rock that was harder than the object being shaped and finished. It's fun for me to think that several different schools of caveman grinding technology evolved. I'm almost sure there were some who preferred a round stone and others who were of the square or rectangular persuasion.

To prepare the forged blade for heat-treating I used "wet-rocks" which were pieces of broken wheels from old-time foot-powered grinders. I had pieces of two different kinds of sandstone to work with. One stone was coarser than the other was, so I used it to work out the scratches from draw filing. I then went to the finest stone for the finish prior to heat-treated. I measured the grit size of the two stones with a micrometer microscope. The particle size of the coarse stone was .002 to .008 inches, which figures out about 50-grit. The finer stone had a grit size of .001 to .003 inch, which makes the fine stone approximately 80-grit.

The photo shows the proper method of applying the blade to the stone. It took me about eight minutes per side to clean up the file marks. A lot of water is necessary to keep the stones working. If allowed to get too dry the surface of the stone plugs up and becomes inefficient at removing metal. This photo shows the wet-rocks and the

"Stone Age" blade finishing.

The two sandstone rubbing stones, one has a medium-grit size, the other fine. The forged project blade is ready for heat-treating

smoothed up blade that is now ready to be heat-treated.

It would have been easy to cheat and use my belt grinder to smooth up the marks from the grinding wheel but I would have missed a very primal feeling of accomplishment that came over me when I was finished doing it the hard, low-tech, ancient way.

Hand-Finishing With Man-Made Grit

Man-made abrasive grits commonly found are aluminum oxide and silicon carbide. Crystalon, a brand name for silicon carbide stones by Norton, are the best quality I have found. They will cut annealed steel fairly quickly. I start with 120-grit and then go to 240. I then switch to a 320-grit India stone (fine, aluminum oxide) by Norton. After the 320-grit aluminum oxide stone I go to wet or dry paper. An alternative to stone finishing is to go all the way with silicon carbide wet or dry paper.

The Best Hand-Rubbed Finish

The best hand-rubbed finishes are accomplished by alternating directions with the stroke as each grit size gets smaller. See the drawing. This allows any abrasive marks from the previous grit to be more clearly seen. The scratch pattern from the belt will be in direction "B" and the first rub will be lengthwise, "A." See the drawing.

The push stick in use.

CAMI U.S. Listed with nearest FEPA	FEPA (P-Grade) European	MICRON	NEW STRUCTURED (NORaX)	AVERAGE PARTICLE SIZE IN INCHES
600	P 1200	15	/	.00060
500	P 1000	/	/	.00071
400	P 800	30	A 25	.00085
360	P 600	/	A 35	.00100
320	P 400	40	A 45	.00137
/	P 320	/	A 60	.00180
240	/	/	A 65	.00209
/	P 240	60	A 75	.00254
220	/	/	A 90	.00257
180	P 180	80	A 110	.00304
150	/	100	/	.00378
120	/	/	A 160	.00452
/	P 100	/	A 200	.00608
80	P 80	/	/	.00768
60	60	/	/	.01014

Grit size conversion table.

hand. Silicon carbide, wet or dry paper is used, some use water and some use it dry. Dry is always best for the final steps. Grit sizes are rounded off to the nearest hundred-something, use what ever you can find available. The push stick can be 1/2-inch or 1-inch wide; the abrasive paper is cut accordingly. A narrow face allows more pressure to be applied; the wide one will work out divots better. My advice is to try the 1-inch-wide stick first.

The final step is always in direction "A" with all the strokes starting at the tang and going towards the point.

The hand-rubbing process may be accomplished by alternating directions "A" and "B" only but there may be scratches left from a previous grit that are hard to see.

When the finishing is being done without a grinder the sequence would be as follows. "A" would be 100- to 120-grit, "B" would be 200, and back to "A" for 300, "B" would be 400 and so on till the desired degree of finish is achieved. To further refine the final steps "C" and "D" can also be utilized.

I use what I call a push stick for hand-rubbing. (See the photo.) It will be good to experiment with a variety of grit sizes and push sticks with surfaces made of different materials until you get the finish you like. I have push sticks faced with wood, steel, leather and rubber of different types. There are times when I use paper as fine as 2,000-grit (FEPA). (See the grit size conversion chart.) It is necessary to have a firm and flat surface backing the paper; the one shown is made of Micarta. The abrasive paper is wrapped around the push stick and held with the

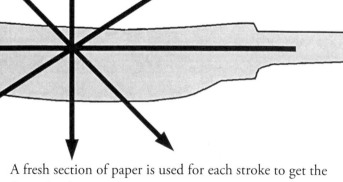
The sequence for hand-rubbing.

A fresh section of paper is used for each stroke to get the finest finish.

The Quick Hand-Rubbed Finish

I used what I call a quick-rubbed finish on many forged blades that are intended for hard use. It's quick because the strokes are all lengthwise with the blade. The quick-rubbed finish results in a nice, although not perfect, finish because there are usually some coarser lines under the final finish. The trick is to keep the scratch pattern all going in the same direction.

When using a belt grinder to start the finishing process, the blade can be taken anywhere from 300 to

The satin finishing buffer with compound.

600-grit before the hand-finishing starts. I stop at 320. Whatever the final belt grit size, the hand-finishing starts by dropping back one grit-size coarser to start.

How To Do A Machine-Made Satin Finish

The satin finish shows its pattern at a 90-degree angle to the edge and is usually not much finer than 300- to 400-grit with light buffing. Here's how I do my version of a satin finish. I work the blade down to a half-dull, 240-grit finish, or if you prefer use a sharp 320 belt. The blade can be flat, convex or hollow ground. Carefully buff the blade with No. SF (satin finishing) 220- or 300-grit compound. I use the compound on a 10-inch sewn muslin wheel that runs 1,750 rpm. It takes practice to get a uniform scratch pattern. At this point the surface will be fairly open and not too smooth. The next step is to buff the blade lightly with a medium cutting compound. Easy does it with this step, once or twice down each side is enough. Finish the blade by buffing lightly once or twice down each side with a finish compound like RCH Green Chrome. Over-buffing with the final finish compound will wipe out the scratch pattern that sets up the satin finish. The result will be a shiny blade. The finish buffing is done on a different 10-inch, sewn muslin wheel that runs at 1,750 rpm. With practice you will be able to get a nice, not-too-shiny, satin finish.

Satin finishing compound is a water-base glue product that is also called greaseless compound. It is applied to the wheel while it is turning. I turn the buffer on, then turn it off and apply the compound as the wheel runs down. Not too much is required. If the compound is applied in a thick layer the buff acts more like a grinding wheel and it will not make a good looking satin finish. The wheel is left running until the glue-based compound hardens. That will take 15 minutes or more depending on the humidity and temperature. These compounds are available from most knifemaker supply companies.

The Mirror Finish

When making knives for the collector market it is probably desirable to learn to mirror polish blades. However, the highest quality knives being sold today usually have hand-rubbed finishes. Blades that are not stainless steel benefit from a high polish because the surface is smoother and more resistant to rust and staining. The main disadvantage of a high polish is it is hard to maintain (keep shiny and scratch free). I made a lot of stock-removal, highly polished blades back in the 1970s. I observed how traumatic it was to a customer when they accidentally scratched their shiny blade. Some were almost afraid to use and sharpen their knives for fear of spoiling the finish, and some of them did just that. I rarely mirror polish because I prefer the appearance and practicality of a satin or hand-rubbed finish. Satin finished blades don't show every little scratch like a mirror polished blade and are very easy to touch-up.

When I do mirror polish a blade I first hand-rub it to about 800-grit, then go to the buffing wheels. Buffing is done like hand rubbing, using all the angles. The only angle you don't want to use is where you stick the cutting edge into the buff. There are many different compounds available from knifemaker supply companies. The important thing is that the step in grit size from one to the next is not too great. The supplier will usually be able to tell you which ones to buy. I use two compounds, one cutting (grayish black) and the other very fine (green). I've had them so long I don't really know exactly where I got them or what they are called. Each compound has its own wheel. I run 10-inch diameter buffs at 1,750 rpm, anything faster than that is too dangerous for me.

The Most Dangerous Machine in the Knife Shop

The buffer gets my vote because it has the habit of grabbing blades and throwing them right back at the person who stuck it into the wheel. Buffer safety starts with the way it is mounted to the bench. In my opinion it is not safe to have a buffer sitting directly on a table or bench. The buffer base should be set on a board that is out from the bench. The reason is that any thing that is tossed down by the inertia of the wheel can bounce back and then be propelled by the wheel in the direction of the operator. Several layers of carpet or one of rubber conveyor belting on the floor under the buffer will protect any object propelled down by the wheel. It will also keep blades from bouncing as high as they do when they hit the cement at 80 miles per hour. I was holding a folding knife blade with my bare fingers to buff off the wax used in the logo etching process. The blade was caught by the wheel, made the trip to the cement floor and bounced up directly into the face of the wheel. The blade was again propelled to the cement and bounced up again, however, this time the point of the blade stuck in my fat little finger. It was then that I decided it was more intelligent to hold blades during that process with ViseGrip® pliers.

I run stitched buffs that start out 10 inches in diameter at 1,750 rpm. Running at 3,400 rpm will do the job faster but the added danger is not worth it for me. I'll run a 6-inch wheel at 3,400, but nothing larger. The reason for using the stitched buffs is that they aren't as grabby as loose buffs. I keep about the last two rows of stitches cut so that the surface is not so hard. There are times when a hard face is desirable, but most of the time a softer edge is better for getting in corners where the guard meets the blade.

I dress my wheels at an angle because it makes it easier to get the corner of the wheel into tight places. (See the drawing.) It also allows more "reach" with longer work pieces. Before mounting, a new wheel has the corner cut off with a huge pair of scissors made to cut carpet. Once mounted, the wheel is dressed with a rake made by driving nails through a piece of plywood. The scissors will then be used to smooth it up again before it is run.

Knives with a double guard are probably the most dangerous to buff. My habit is to have everything finished prior to attaching the guard and that eliminates serious buffing after assembly. A friend who I taught to make knives got in a hurry and mounted his buffer directly on a bench. A dagger got caught by the guard, bounced off the table back into the wheel, was propelled around and directly through the palm of his hand. The interesting part of this story is that he had a helper take a photo of the mess before pulling it out. It took $3,000 and several months of recovery before he was back to work. (That $3,000. was at mid-1970s prices.)

The buffer should have a guard over it. Even if nothing is ever propelled around the wheel and into your face it is nice to have the fluff and excess compound going down to the floor instead of in your face. My guards are made out of plywood, glued and screwed together. My theory is that a knife blade propelled around the wheel might stick into the wood before it gets to me. A lip at the front of the guard can be adjustable so that it can be lowered when the wheel gets worn down.

Sand-Blasted Finishes

This is a popular thing for tactical knives. The finish prior to sandblasting should be uniform over the surface of the blade. Heavy sandblasting with coarse sand will blend in some scratches but won't hide them all. Fine or dull sand will have less effect on the surface finish. Pick a method to give the visual effect that you want for the blade. A tactical folder might look better with a fine satin finish lightly blasted. A rough and ready survival knife might look just fine with a 120- or 220 grit belt finish with a heavy blast job.

A sandblasted finish leaves the skin of the blade open to attack of any corrosive elements. It would be good to keep a non-stainless blade with a sandblasted finish well oiled.

The Full-Tang Knife

Fitting the handle on a full-tang knife without the use of power equipment is a real challenge. The knife I made for the magazine series had handle slabs of Oregon-grown maple burl that came out of my neighbors scrap pile. It had been run through a planer so I had two smooth sides to start with and that made it easier. All I had to do was split the piece with a saw and put the flat sides next to the tang. I used a nickel-alloy brazing rod for pin stock and Devcon five-minute epoxy as a seal between the handle and tang.

The finishing sequence is as follows:
- Drawfile the tang to get it very flat. (Keep the disk sander off of the tang or else it won't stay flat.)
- Finish the blade with a disk attachment on the electric drill and hand rub to an 800-grit finish.
- Flatten the handle slabs if necessary and work them down to the thickness you want for the handle. Check to make sure they are the same thickness and parallel. To get the full-tang handle slabs flat I used

wood-rasps and the "Backwoods" belt sander that as shown in photo.
- Drill the holes in the handle slabs: I confused myself as I tried to describe this sequence so I'll explain "front" and "back". When a knife is described it should have the edge down and the point to the left. The surface you see is the front and the hidden side is the back. The tang would normally have been drilled prior to heat-treating Lay the outer surface of the slab for the front of the knife on the back-side of the tang and drill one

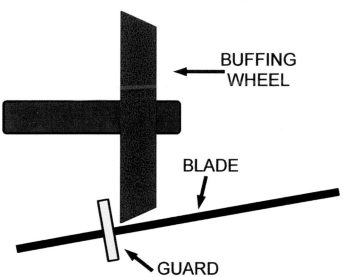

This illustration shows the advantage of dressing a buffing or grinding wheel at an angle so as to give clearance for long work.

This is the safe buffing setup, nothing under the wheels but the floor with its rubber pad.

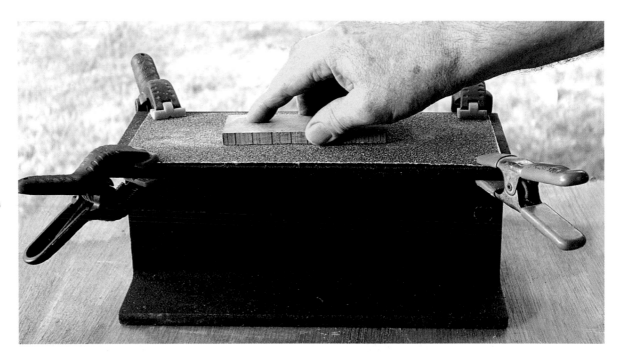

The backwoods belt sander.

The drilling machine from the dumpster.

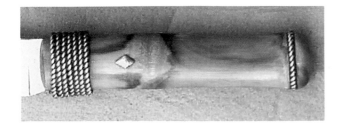

You have probably noticed the bamboo that makes the background for many of my photos. Here you have a handle made with material from my bamboo farm. It's a very hard wood with lots of color.

hole, place a trial pin in that hole and drill the second hole. Then turn the blade over and drill the clamped-into-position slab for the back of the knife, once again using the holes in the tang for a guide. Placing a trial pin in the first drilled hole keeps the slab from slipping out of position from the pressure created when the drill bit first contacts the wood. Drilling the wood slabs from the outer surface, using the tang holes for a guide keeps any chipping of the wood hidden in the final assembly. My drilling machine was the rusted up drill-press adapter for an electric hand drill. I rescued it from a dumpster at a moving sale. I assume the person who trashed it thought it might not work because of the rust, however, all it needed was some WD-40 and some fine sandpaper to get it loosened up.

• Clamp the handle slabs together with the trial pins in place and shape and finish the edges on the blade end. If you do the glue-up with the slabs uneven on the blade end you'll never be able to match them up.

• Check the fit and alignment by placing the slabs on the tang with the trial pins in place. If all is well then proceed with the glue-up.

• Mix the epoxy carefully as per the instructions and make sure it is above 70 degrees F. If epoxy is mixed when cold it may not reach the full strength it is capable of. Work the trial pins out before the epoxy is fully hardened. Wear rubber gloves and use some acetone to clean out the holes. When the epoxy has cured run a sharp drill through the holes to clean out any excess epoxy.

• Cut the pin stock to length (slightly longer than the thickness of the handle), then rough up the pins with coarse sandpaper and lock them in place with super-glue. You might want to experiment with using the final pins in the glue-up and skip the super-glue step. Use care when working the excess pin material down even with the wood, get it too hot and it will make a ring of burnt wood around the pin.

• Shape and smooth up the handle with sandpaper, taking it down to 320-grit, then work it over with the finest steel wool you can find, 0000 or finer. Stain it with wood stain or leather dye if desired and treat with Deft Danish Oil finish or some other wood sealer/finish. I like to apply the finish over a three-day period. Maple will absorb a lot of a wet,

penetrating finish like Deft. When no more will soak in, the handle is lightly worked all over with the finest steel wool, and then rubbed to a high shine with an old wool sock. This finish is in the wood and not on the surface and that's the way is should be for a knife handle.

• Sharpen your new knife and then use it to cut something so that you can experience the satisfaction of using a tool that you created with your own hands.

Stock-Removal Project Completed

The combination of handle and blade shape is one I've made in a variety of sizes for more than 30 years. It's called a patch knife, little hunting knife or a letter opener; it just depends on who is using it at the time.

The Narrow-Tang Forged Knife

The narrow-tang blade forged from a Honda automobile coil spring was finished without the use of electricity. The handle was also finished by hand without the use of any power tools. I used a tree branch from my dad's yard for a handle and a scrap piece of copper pipe for a ferrule or bolster.

The tree branch was cut roughly to length. The narrow tang was heated to around 500 to 600 degrees F and worked into the handle material. This is called, "burning in the tang" and is probably the oldest method of putting a handle on a knife. If wood is stubborn, grind a long, square-section taper on an old file or any other steel that is handy. A small chisel tip on the end will help the burning process when the burning tool is turned and pushed at the same time. Every so often you should let the burning process rest. If you get the handle material too hot it can crack. Go slow as the tang gets close to being fully burned into the handle. With this type of construction there was no need for a belt grinder or drill press. Nature furnishes many excellent handle materials in a round form. I used a section of tree branch because the only shaping required was some work with files and sandpaper. This is much less labor intensive than cutting the whole tree down, making boards out of it and then cutting the handle out of one of the boards.

The handle material is held in a simple wooden jig that is clamped in the vise jaws. The coarse cutting file has had the teeth ground off of the side that rests on the wood jig. The photo shows the file forming the shoulder for the ferrule. The tip of the file has been ground so that it will

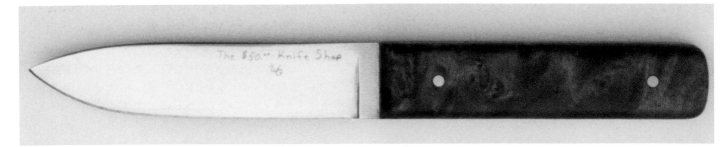

The finished stock-removal knife made from the lawnmower blade.

get down in the cavity that the tang will go into.

The section of copper tube can be put on as a parallel ferrule but better yet it is enlarged on the handle end with a tapered punch. I used a tapered punch ground from a piece of round bar stock to form a slight taper in the ferrule. Whichever way is used, the handle is shaped so that the ferrule has to be driven on the last fraction of an inch. This wedges everything up tight, the tang in the handle and the ferrule onto the handle.

The handle material was very close to the finished size so very little shaping was necessary. When everything was smoothed up the handle was given a coat of penetrating finish. Deft and Watco are my favorites.

The Finished Product

The finished knife is resting on the world's smallest forge. Along with it are the remainder of the copper tube and a piece of the handle material. At the top of the picture you can see part of a coil spring from a 1981 Honda Accord, it's the mate to the one I cut up to use for the project knife. Although the knife won't win any beauty contests it is a solid hard-working cutting tool that used an absolute minimum of tools to make.

The forged knife ended up with an unconventional configuration of handle and blade, that's because not too many knives have the blade offset from the handle. This is an advantage when cutting vegetables on a cutting board. There are two reasons why the handle came out off-center. First of all was it was sloppy forging on my part that left the tang above the centerline of the blade. Second, the process of burning-in the tang to fit the handle resulted in the hole in the handle being off center. I looked at it and said "why not," and went ahead and affixed the handle to the blade with the copper ferrule made of water pipe. Don't be afraid to make your own rules about how you do things. However, you should probably rethink your rules if no one ever buys one of your knives.

Shoulder filing jig for fitting the ferrule to the handle.

As I finished the first edition of this book the knife had been used for over a year. I used it for a variety of tasks and found the blade shape and size very handy in the yard, shop and kitchen. The only problem I have with it is the nearly round handle; it has the tendency to turn in the hand on heavy whittling type cuts. (That serves me right for being cheap and using a tree branch for a knife handle.) A better handle shape is rectangular in cross section with just the corners are rounded off, this gives a secure grip on the knife with less chance of it turning in the hand.

All About Tangs

The majority of knives and swords throughout history have had narrow tangs. The many advantages of the narrow tang became clear from my experiments with primitive knifemaking methods. When forging a blade it is much easier to shape a narrow tang than to work out a full tang. It takes almost twice as much steel to make a full-tang knife hunting size as it does to make one with a narrow tang. Steel was a valuable commodity and undoubtedly the frugality of bladesmiths helped to prompt the perfection of the narrow tang.

Let's think about all the available materials that are found in the shape of a knife handle. Bones, antler parts, horns, tusks and tree branches of the correct diameter are all ready to be fitted onto a tang. The handle material surrounds the narrow tang and that makes a lot less metal to be finished when compared to a full tang. Another

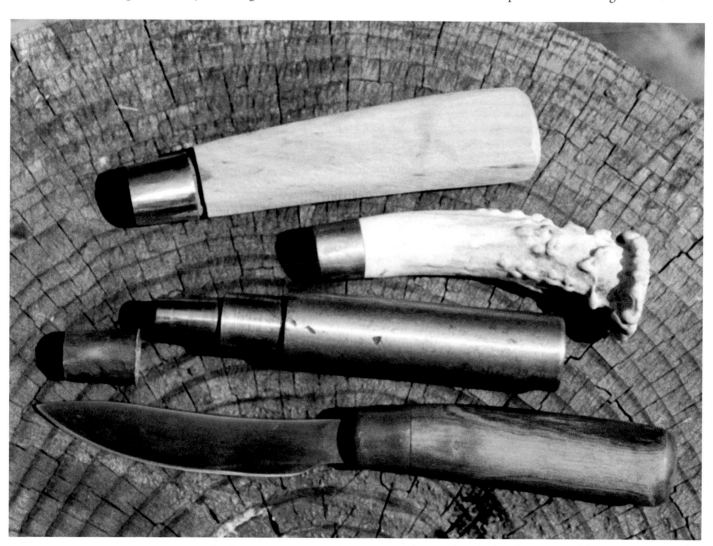

Top, a rough handle of chinquapin from a firewood pile that has been fitted for a copper ferrule. Chinquapin, genus Castanopsis is an evergreen tree found in the Pacific Northwest. It is light tan colored, about the hardness of maple or walnut. Second from top is a deer antler that has been fitted with a copper cap. This type of ferrule requires a bit more work to make the hole for the tang but gives a smooth and attractive transition where the blade comes out of the handle. The tapered punch used to form the ferrule is next to a piece of scrap copper tubing. At the bottom is the forged blade from The $50 Knife Shop Series. The handle had been stained and the knife seen some use by the time this picture was taken.

The forged project is finished, note the bare, untreated handle.

factor to consider is the fact that the narrow-tang knife is a sealed unit compared to slab handles affixed to a full tang. There is no doubt in my mind that there are fewer things that can go wrong with a properly constructed narrow-tang knife. A final point is that narrow-tang construction has always been common because few tools were required and it is the most logical way to make a knife.

Most of the opinions I hear regarding tang strength are hypothetical in nature and not based on experience making knives of both types. I made both tang types for a long time without really considering the differences in strength or durability. Over the years I've had less trouble with narrow-tang handles than with full-tang versions. That's why it's my opinion that when properly constructed

the narrow tang is the strongest and most foolproof handle. It must be done right or it might not be any better than a full-tang model. My opinion is also based on the most severe test of tang strength that I have been able to devise. I drove the point of a knife through a 2 by 4 board by pounding on the pommel cap with a 4-pound hammer. The knife had a wire-damascus blade, Micarta handle with a steel guard and pommel cap. The properly constructed narrow tang will withstand this type of abuse. I'd never try it with a slab-handled full-tang knife.

Why Tangs Fail

The strength of the tang is often overlooked as a design element. I've seen many knives and a couple of swords that had broken in the tang area. Seeing what went wrong has caused me to form some strong opinions about how a tang should be constructed.

Broken tangs can result from defective heat treatment. The steel in the tang could be either too hard or too soft. When it is too soft it can bend; too hard and it will break. Spring temper is the best condition for a tang to be in.

When a handle breaks at the junction of the blade and guard it is usually because of a stress riser. A square corner at the junction of blade and tang causes the stress riser. The stress of the quenching process is concentrated in the square corner and it can cause a crack to form. It's an accident waiting to happen because even if a crack didn't start during the quenching process, the stress riser could cause unexpected failure during use. That corner should have as large a radius as is feasible. See the drawing.

The handle material in a failed tang might have been too weak for the intended purpose. Spacer-type handles require extra material in the tang to make up for the lack of strength in the cross section of the handle material. Air space between the tang and handle material can allow the handle to shift on the tang. This will also cause extra stress that could break a knife at the tang.

One last thing that can cause a tang to fail is the grain structure of the steel. During a 2 by 4 chop for the ABS Journeyman test, the blade broke at the junction with the tang. The steel in the tang didn't appear to be too hard but it did have an extremely coarse grain from being overheated in a coal forge. There is an ever-present danger of ruining the steel by overheating when working with coal. The average gas forge used for bladesmithing won't get hot enough to damage the steel.

The test was failed so whatever I did with the broken knife was only for the edification of the applicant and myself. I wanted to finish the test to see what the quality of the blade was so I reattached the tang with a silver-brazed joint and proceeded with the test procedures. See the photo. The applicant should have learned one big lesson, and that is to not go to a test without first testing the knife.

Silver Brazing

I learned to silver-braze many years ago when I worked in the saw manufacturing and repair business. My first job

Wire damascus knife with maximum-strength handle construction.

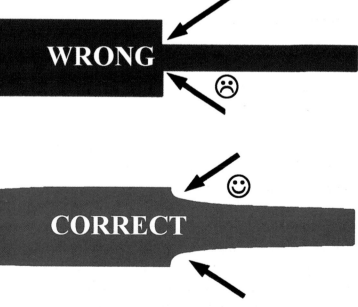

Be sure to make your tangs with a nice radius as shown in the illustration. Do not do it wrong and have a sad experience.

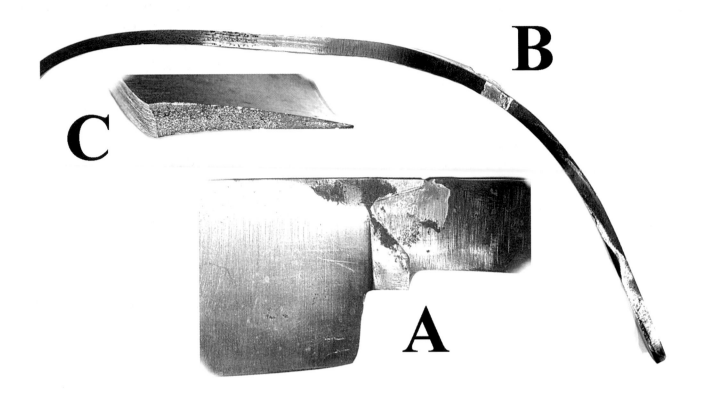

The broken knife mentioned in the text was repaired by silver brazing the tang back onto the blade. Note the tongue and groove fit. The test continued with the following results. The edge bent slightly on the 2 by 4 chop. The tip broke off in the flex test. Note the coarse grain. (The grain in the tang was even coarser.) The remainder of the blade, minus the tip, survived a 90-degree flex. The silver braze joint held up through the whole ordeal.

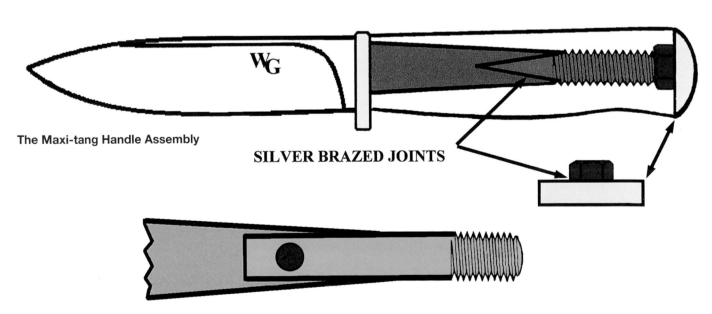

The Maxi-tang Handle Assembly

SILVER BRAZED JOINTS

Details of a riveted tang extension.

was silver-brazing carbide bits into saws and cutters of all descriptions. It is an excellent process to master because it can be used to repair all kinds of steel items that no other method would do as well.

Silver-brazing is sometimes confused with silver-soldering. The distinctions are made by the differences in the melting points of the solder and braze materials. Silver brazing is a higher-temperature process, usually greater than 900 degrees F. Silver-soldering is usually accomplished at 430 degrees F, which results in a rather weak joint when, compared to silver brazing. The silver-brazing rod I use melts at around 1,300 degrees F, and results in a joint that is stronger than the two pieces of steel that it joins. Check with your local welding supply store for medium- or high-strength silver-brazing rod and temperature-matched flux. They should have product information sheets with the instructions available for the asking.

The advantage of silver-brazing a tang extension as opposed to welding is that the grain structure of the steel is not enlarged. This is because the temperature to braze is lower than the transformation point of the steel. I use a "V" joint and silver-braze the tang on after the guard is pushed in place for the last time. That way I can have a 3/8-inch threaded end cap on a blade with a 3/16- or 1/4-inch thick blade. After brazing, the tang is subjected to a double spring temper. I'd use a propane torch to slowly bring the color up through blue going into silver. The time at temperature in a tempering operation can have an effect on the finished strength. Doing it twice not only gives the part more total time at the tempering temperature but also equals it out in case it was not uniform the first time. Spring temper in most steel types is from 44 to 50 HRC.

To add a pommel cap, a nut of the correct size to match the tang extension is silver-brazed to the pommel material. The handle can be drawn up tight and there is no thread showing.

Another method to use on small knives is to silver-braze a wood screw to the butt cap. The butt cap w/screw attached is then screwed and glued into the handle material. A good silver solder job would probably hold the screw to the pommel cap on light-duty knives but I wouldn't trust it on a heavy-use knife. I've seen several knives where the butt caps were attached with epoxy and the caps eventually fell off.

Arc Welded Tangs

This has to be done with great skill or else the joint will fail. When I welded on tang extensions (even though they were tempered back) they were often weak because of a coarse grain structure. This is the normal result of the high temperatures required for arc or gas welding. I never got the type of strength that I wanted. I'm no welder either, but with steels like O-1 and 52100 which air-harden, it is more trouble than it is worth. Even if you get the weld zone springy it is coarse-grained and weak. An arc or gas welded joint might be strong enough if it was forged and normalized, then given a blue temper. This will give better strength to the welded joint but it will never have the strength of a silver brazed joint.

Riveted Tangs

Some sword makers use a riveted connection. I've used it on knives and see no reason why it can't be adequately strong when done correctly. As stated above, the strength in a narrow-tang handle with a pommel cap is dependent on the size and spring temper in the tang. All of it has to be drawn up tight by the pommel cap with no air gaps that might allow the handle material to shift on the tang. See the drawing.

CHAPTER 4

BACKYARD HEAT TREATING

Low-Tech

Was it James Black of Washington, Arkansas, or someone else who made the knife that helped to propel James Bowie onto the pages of history? Whoever it was, he certainly did not understand martensite or austenite. These two forms of steel, relative to heat-treating, had not been identified and named at that time. The knifemakers of the early 1800s wouldn't have known what was meant by upper or lower critical temperatures or understood how to read a nose curve. They did understand that properly prepared steel would get hard when heated to a certain color and quenched in a suitable liquid. The hard and brittle steel would then be heated to a lower "tempering" temperature in order to soften it just enough to be serviceable. This knowledge had been learned by trial and error and passed down from generation to generation. Heat-treating in the early 1800s was certainly primitive by the standards of the today, however, it was more than adequate to "win the West" and make history.

In November 1987 I traveled to the shop of W. F. Moran for my ABS Master Smith test. I passed it with a blade that was heat treated with what can be called backyard methods. A magnet was used to judge the correct temperature and then it was quenched in goop and tempered with a soft back draw. I passed and we were both happy with the results of the test. I received my Master Smith rating after passing the board of judges in May 1988.

TIME-TEMPERATURE DIAGRAM

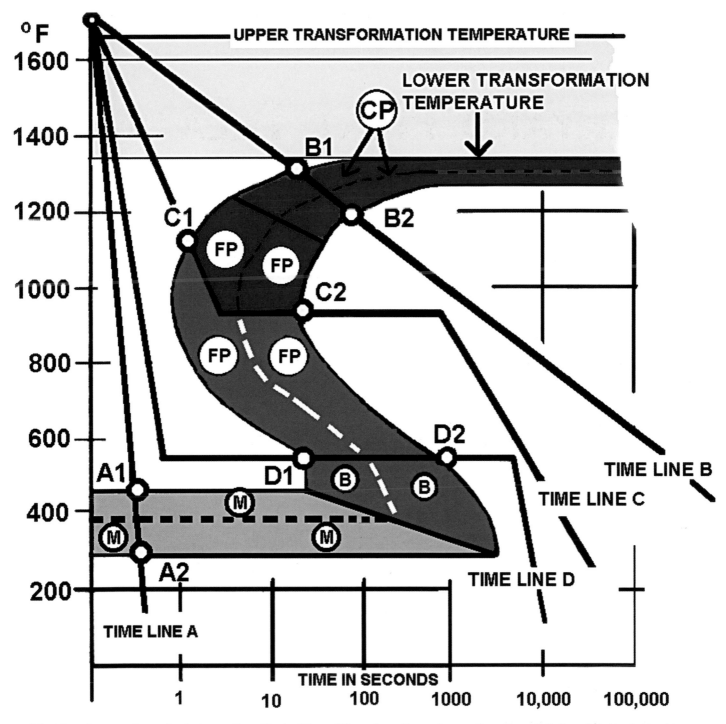

The time-temperature chart shows the effect of four different cooling rates as time lines A,B,C and D. Each steel type has its own unique "nose" curve which is determined by quenching sample pieces of the steel type at different cooling rates.

In order for steel to become fully hard it must be cooled fast enough to miss the nose of the curve as in time line A. This time line results in martensite, which is the hardest transformation product of steel. Martensite has to be tempered to make a serviceable blade.

Time line B is the slowest cooling and results in the soft structure coarse pearlite. Coarse pearlite is a combination of coarse pearlite, coarse ferrite and coarse cementite.

Time line C causes the steel to have the structure fine pearlite. Time line D causes the steel to transform to bainite. Bainite is more ductile than martensite and is a good compromise between the softer structures ferrite, cementite, or pearlite and brittle martensite.

High-tech

Today we find many knifemakers using digitally controlled electric furnaces for heat-treating their blades. Those who want to heat-treat their stainless steel blades will not be able to get by without the addition of a Rockwell test machine and a container for the liquid nitrogen for the freeze treating operation. There is a growing trend among bladesmiths to use high-temperature salt pots to heat for quenching and a lower-temperature salt bath for tempering. Twenty-years ago none of us thought that those things were necessary. Rockwell test machines have replaced the file for hardness testing in many knifemakers' shops. The craft of making handmade knives is becoming more "high-tech" with each passing year.

I hope the mention of the high-tech heat-treating equipment will not discourage anyone from using what I like to call "Backyard Heat Treating." The lesson is presented because I, and many others, use simple equipment and methods to make very excellent knives from carbon and carbon alloy steels.

The other side of the coin is that some makers using high-tech heat-treating equipment are turning out knives that haven't reached the full potential of the steel. Hardness testers can get out of calibration; incorrect times and temperatures might be used. Worst of all, not many makers do any testing to see if what they did to the blade works in real-life cutting situations. A vital part of the heat-treating process is testing and that is covered at the end of this section.

The hardening/tempering formula given to you by another may not be correct with the way you do things. Your quench may make the blade harder or softer; this means that you may have to adjust the tempering cycle to get a proper hardness. The only way you can have confidence in your heat-treating process, be it high tech or low tech is to have some type of testing program. Testing is basically comparing the performance of your blades against blades of known value. See the section describing the brass rod test.

The broken blade described in the section on silver brazing was the result of a maker not working out the proper heat treat process with his equipment. Plus, he must not have done any testing of blades produced by his process. The test blade obviously had not been tested.

Judging The Proper Hardening Temperature With A Magnet

I may never have learned that I couldn't judge the proper temperature for hardening by eye if I had not been working on my American Bladesmith Society requirements. Some of my test blades broke and the break showed a coarse grain structure. (Grain size can't actually be seen with the naked eye, what is seen is the crystal size and that is an indication of the grain size.) I knew enough metallurgy to know that overheated steel when quenched can have a coarse grain. I believed that I was overheating some of the blades. I had heard about judging the hardening temperature with a magnet and so I tried it and had no more broken blades because of a coarse grain. The ability of steel to attract a magnet at room temperature is a very useful one. The fact that steel loses that attraction as it reaches the critical temperature is extremely useful for the backyard bladesmith/knifemaker.

The blade is heated slowly and uniformly until a magnet no longer is attracted to it, the heat is allowed to rise another 50 degrees or so and then the blade is quenched. My preference in magnets for heat-treating are the pocket-sized, telescoping type available at most places where tools are sold. I recently found some at a "Dollar" store and at Harbor Freight.

.As the temperature of steel increases, the atoms vibrate about their usual position and that generates light that is emitted from the surface. Each discernible color is an indication of a specific temperature in that type of steel; however, the color seen will vary depending on the available light. In order to accurately judge the temperature for hardening by color alone it is necessary to have the light conditions as close to identical as possible for each session. The traditional hardening temperature color is "cherry red" (1,475 degrees F or thereabouts). The temperature indicated by any color as seen in a dark shop appears quite different in a location with more light. My smithy is open on three sides and well illuminated by natural light during most of the year. I cannot trust my color judgment for hardening under those conditions and using a magnet allows me to get consistent results. I cannot recommend color judgment by eye for the beginner, and I've seen some experienced smiths be fooled by it.

Quenchants for Hardening

There is nothing fancy or expensive required here. Most any oil or combination of oils will work. In order to obtain full hardness simple steels need to be cooled from the hardening temperature to around 400 degrees F in somewhere between two and eight seconds. The cooling rate necessary for hardening changes with the number and percentage of the alloy elements. The method of cooling does not matter as long as the time/temperature rate is achieved. See the time-temperature-transformation diagram.

Water Quenching

Water will work if it is done carefully but I do not use it, nor do I recommend it for a beginner. Never quench a blade in water unless the steel didn't respond to an oil quench. If you do decide to water quench, heat the water to between 90 and 140 degrees F, stick the blade in for about a second, pull it out and put it right back in for another second or two, then repeat the process. It's risky business but may be the only way to harden some blades. If the blade still doesn't harden, try cold water and then brine. If that doesn't work, find some other type of steel. When used for knives, the water-hardening steels (W-1 and W-2) should be quenched in oil. Water quenching of any thin object like the edge of a knife may cause cracking or excess warping.

Safety First With Quench Baths

Following are steps you should observe to ensure a safe quench:

- The quenchant should be in a spill-proof container with an airtight lid.
- Always wear leather gloves when quenching in case of a flame-up.
- Keep the cover available to smother the fire if the oil flames up.
- Tongs can be dangerous to use if they're allowed to heat up along with the blade. Hot tongs can cause the oil to flame up because they act just like a candlewick. A good safety measure is to use one pair of tongs to hold the blade while heating and then grab the hot blade with a cold pair of tongs just prior to the quench.
- When doing a full hardening quench always hang the blade on a wire so that it can be lowered straight and point first into the oil. Use the tongs to manipulate it in the furnace or forge fire, but use the wire when quenching.
- Always have a deep enough bath to completely submerge the heated part of the blade. Leaving any portion of the heated blade above the surface of the oil will cause the oil to flame up. The exception to this is the edge quench and

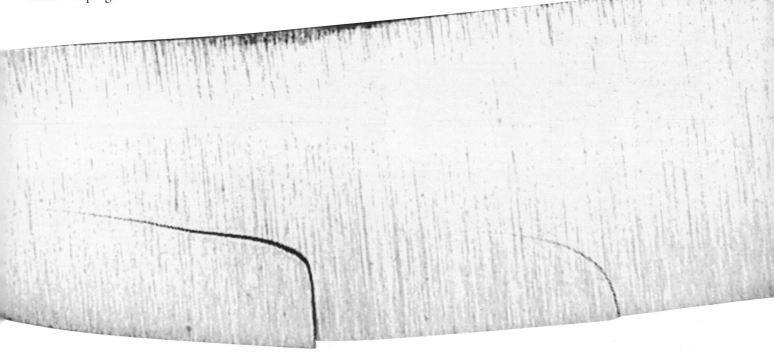

The two cracks are typical of what happens to an oil hardening steel if it is edge quenched in water. A full quench would have resulted in the cracks going straight up on the blade. The edge quench caused the crack to follow the water line.

you will have to put up with a certain amount of flame.

- Keep a thermometer in the oil to monitor the temperature. Stop quenching if the temperature gets over 180 degrees F.
- Use a large enough container to do the desired number of blades without the oil overheating. Two gallons of oil will do between six to eight average-size knives with no trouble.

Thermal Treatments For The Forged Blade

The four common operations in the heat-treating process are normalizing, annealing, hardening and tempering. The bladesmith adds one more because I consider the finishing heat on a forged blade as a thermal treatment. The success of the heat treatment will depend on the condition of the steel before the quench process. This is where thermal treatments come into the story. Blades that are forged need to be normalized, but not necessarily annealed. Two or three normalizing cycles may

be better than one so it's good to experiment with the steel you are working with. Annealing is necessary if the normalized blade is too hard to file or drill. I always anneal so that I will be able to easily straighten out any bends or kinks. Once the blade is straight and true it will get a final normalizing treatment.

The Finishing Heat

If you were to watch me forge a blade you might assume that I was packing it. (See the section on packing that follows annealing.) My finishing heat looks a lot like packing but I don't call it that. Metallurgy theory calls it a "finishing heat" so I'll stick with that.

I will assume that your blade is pretty well shaped and that proper measures were taken to not overheat it or leave it with a lot of scale hammered into the surface. The finishing heat means working the blade over with light and even hammer blows down into the temperature range where there is little or no color visible. This will leave the blade smooth and relatively clean and free of scale. The light blows do not move the steel or change the shape very

I overheated a large bronze bushing while forging it down to guard size. When I pulled it out of the forge the end I'd been forging on stayed in there. The piece that fell off showed the coarse grain at the bottom. I heated the end of the remaining piece to a black heat, quenched in water, (annealing for bronze) notched it and broke it to see the result of the grain refinement. You can see the comparison between it and the end of the piece that fell off in the forge.

much but serve to even out the surface. If there are still rough and uneven places or scale on the surface, heat it up to a temperature that is just under the point where scale forms and do the light hammering once more.

Normalizing

When the finishing heat is complete, the blade is ready to be normalized. Normalizing is necessary to refine the grain structure and relieve the uneven stresses set up in the blade during the forging process. Normalizing is accomplished by heating the blade slowly and uniformly to a point just a little past where a magnet is not attracted to it. The blade is then removed from the heat and allowed to cool in still air. If you are the technical type, the correct temperature for normalizing 5160 steel is 1,600 degrees F. As soon as the blade has reached the temperature of the air it is ready to be annealed.

When I started forging all I knew was to anneal after the final forging heat. It would be hard to say what the structures of my blades were prior to the quench process. A lot of my blades warped badly when quenched. After I started normalizing, I didn't have much of a problem with warping. I don't know that it's possible to heat treat blades and not have some that warp. One old blacksmith book says that if you are going to make knives you will have to learn how to straighten them, and the writer was certainly correct. See chapter 8, the three-point straightening jigs I use are shown there.

Grinding the blade to its final dimensions takes place either between the normalizing and annealing or after annealing. When the blade is hot it is difficult to see how straight it is. I will often rough-grind a blade, especially the larger ones, after normalizing. If there is any major problem with kinks or twists in the blade it will go back into a medium hot fire, just under critical, and straighten the blade as necessary. The blade is then normalized again and then it is ready for annealing.

Annealing

The following works for simple steels. The blade is heated slowly and uniformly to where it just loses its ability to attract a magnet. (1,525 degrees F for 5160) The blade is then put in warm ashes or vermiculite and allowed to cool slowly to room temperature. It will then be in a soft and stress-free condition, perfect for whatever stock removal needs to be done. Annealing, as a preparatory treatment

prior to the quenching process, may not be necessary with all types of steel. Check with the steel maker's specification sheets to see what is recommended. Be sure to ask for the heat-treating information whenever you purchase steel, it is available and the supplier should furnish it to the purchaser.

Chromium steel, 52100, has a very complicated annealing cycle, it requires a cycle anneal as follows. Heat to 1,440 degrees F for eight hours, cool 15 degrees per hour to 1,200 degrees, and hold that temperature for six hours, then cool in still air. In case you haven't figured it out, that will require a digitally controlled furnace with atmospheric control, or a stainless foil wrap.

What Is Packing?

Packing is a process that some bladesmiths use in forging blades. The practice came to us out of the 19th century and has been passed down to us by many generations of smiths. Packing is mentioned in many, but not all of the blacksmithing books written in the late 1800s. When it is mentioned it is usually in reference to forging chisels. It is not mentioned very much when forging knife blades is being discussed. It is accepted by some, but questioned by others. As far as I know it has no basis in modern metallurgical theory and I have not found a reference to it in any up-to-date metallurgical books. My 1948 *Metals Handbook* has a definition of "mechanical working" which is a process described as follows. "Subjection metal to pressure exerted by rolls, dies, presses, or hammers, to change its form or to affect the structure and consequently the mechanical and physical properties." When mechanical working is performed at temperatures under critical, it sounds somewhat like packing. An example would be cold-rolled steel. Other modern books on forging practice refer to a "finishing heat" so that's what I teach.

When I got into forging I asked several established bladesmiths to explain their method of packing. Everyone seemed to have his or her own version, but the basic formula was something like this. "Hammering the edge portion of the blade with a light hammer as it cools down to the point that the color is barely visible in a dark place." This doesn't mean hammering on the edge as if you were pushing it back into the blade. The "packing" blows are on the sides of the blade in the edge portion.

The following is how packing is described in print

by a variety of sources: The edge is packed by hammering it lightly to "jiggle" the carbides into alignment. Forging reduces the size of the carbides along the edge surface, while packing tightens the crystal structure so the molecules remain on the knife's edge longer. From another source: The final refinement of the grain size is referred to as "packing" and is done at the same time that the final shape of the bar is finished. Packing the steel is very important and involves hammering the steel at a dull red color for a long period of time. Grain refinement in parallel rows is essential for strong, high-quality cutting edges. The smaller the grain size is, the stronger the material. We have one more opinion: The hammer blows may appear to be random, however, each one is serving a purpose. The grains are being elongated in the direction of maximum stress, somewhat like wood grain. The hammering breaks up large grains and produces a fine-grained, tough, strong structure. As the steel cools out of the red condition, light blows pack the surface and edge. One must be careful at this point, though, because hammering when the steel gets too cool may form cracks.

The "jiggling" part of the above escapes my powers of reasoning. That bladesmith may be confusing carbides, grains, molecules and crystals. I do like the part in the third opinion where it refers to fine grain size being necessary for strength.

While doing my research on packing I asked two different metallurgists what they thought of "packing" theory. Both explained what I already knew, that the steel recrystallizes during the hardening operation. Their opinion was that the temperature of the annealing, normalizing and hardening operation would undo any grain refinement done in the packing process.

It is just fine with me if you want to pack your blade. Be sure that you can explain why you are doing it and what the results will be. And, those results should be backed up by some type of comparison testing of the flexible strength and cutting ability of your blades. You may call it packing if you like, but always remember that the steel will recrystallize in both the normalizing and quench heats. Call it anything you want but I'd rather you don't say that you've jiggled, compressed or lined up the molecules.

None of the old references recommended normalizing; it simply wasn't part of the process back then. The process and what it accomplished to the structure of the steel wasn't understood. Could it be that the packing process was actually leaving the blade in close to a normalized condition? Blades subjected to packing would have had a finer crystal structure from the slow cooling from the transformation temperature. It was a good thing to do. I'm convinced the old timers mistook the results of the thermal treatment caused by the hammer as an effect of the hammer blow.

Thermal Packing

I'm not sure I like the term but it is being used, so I will offer a description of the process. Thermal packing, as it has been described to me, consists of heating the blade to a certain temperature and allowing it to air cool. This temperature is sometimes judged by eye, others determine it with a magnet. (Steel becomes nonmagnetic at the critical [transformation] temperature.) Some smiths who practice thermal packing will speed the cooling of the blade by swinging it around in the air. There are others who let the airflow from a fan cool it. Some believe that two or three treatments are better than one. With some steel types, a single thermal packing may not have any more of an effect than a proper normalizing treatment.

It is important to keep in mind that the many different types of steel forged by bladesmiths will not react the same way to the finishing heat or certain thermal treatments. Carbon content, specific alloy elements and their quantity will all affect the type of structure and grain size at any point in the time/temperature profile of the forged blade. The physical contact between the hot steel, the hammer and anvil that occurs during packing will cool the steel faster than thermal packing, annealing or normalizing. Could it be that the cooling rate caused by the hammering is what causes any difference that may be observed in a finished blade?

Therefore, packing as described above may have an effect on the finished blade because of the time/temperature cycle that takes place during the physical packing with the hammer. The ultra-fine grain that I have observed in ball bearing steel forged with my hydraulic forging press may be the result of the cooling effect of the physical action of the press.

Grain Refinement With Thermal Cycles

See the drawing that shows the results of two different thermal cycles. At the left side of the illustration the grain is refined by heating the metal slightly above the lower critical temperature and then allowing it to cool. When heated above this zone, the grain will again enlarge and with sufficient time at a high temperature will become large and weak as shown by the cooling line at the right of the drawing. Coarse-grained steel is weak. Fine-grained steel is strong. I've never seen a broken test blade that didn't have a coarse grain showing.

Questions To Be Answered

Packing with a hammer puts the grain in a stressed and distorted condition. It is necessary to heat the blade to the recrystallization temperature in order to harden it. What remains after recrystallization of the effects caused by thermal or physical packing?

How do these (possible) changes translate to the properties of flexible strength and edge holding ability in the finished blade?

Does the physical process of forging cause any internal physical changes that remain after recrystallization during the heat-treating process?

If a stock-removal blade receives the same time / temperature treatments as a forged blade, will it have the same size and type of grain structure?

Have the past comparisons between stock removal and forged blades taken into consideration the differences in thermal cycles that the forged blades went through during the forging process?

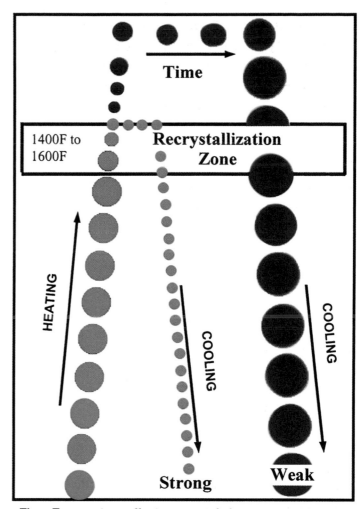

Time-Temperature effect on crystal size.

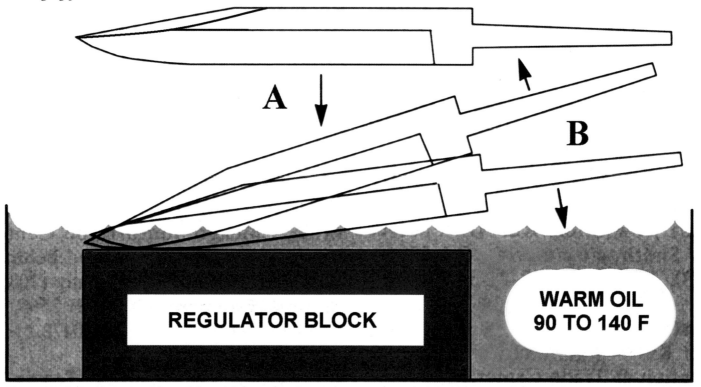

The setup for edge quenching with a regulator block.

It's not a question but something that would be good to remember. It's a fact that steel cannot be compressed or compacted.

Hardening The Blade

The Edge-Quench

After trying every method I ever heard of, I adopted the edge-quench as the superior way to harden any single-edged blade made of carbon or carbon alloy steel. It is easier to learn than the soft back draw and when done correctly, gives a blade excellent flexible strength. I quenched the project knives for *The $50 Knife Shop* series in my "special goop," a mixture of paraffin, cooking fat and hydraulic oil. I used the goop quench in keeping with the intent to use recycled materials whenever possible.

Most any oil will work for the edge-quench. Mineral oil and automatic transmission oil work good, as well as most vegetable oils. A disadvantage of the vegetable oils is that they get rancid. Oils that are specifically made for heat treating have an advantage because they don't flame up as much. On the other hand, the heat treat oils will not necessarily produce a blade that is any harder than the oils mentioned, or for that matter, my "goop" mixture.

The type of oil and its temperature will affect the hardness of the blade. Keeping the temperature of the oil the same each time will make it easier to get consistent results with a given tempering temperature. When oil is used it should be heated to between 90 and 140° F. Cold oil isn't "wet" enough to quench properly. If the oil gets too hot, it may not cool the steel fast enough to make it fully hard. There's also a danger of the oil catching on fire when it gets overheated. Keep a thermometer in the oil and be sure the oil is within the same temperature range each time. A kitchen-type thermometer used for making candy works perfectly.

The most important factor in edge-quenching is getting a proper depth of quench. A combat-quality, unbreakable blade will have about one-third to one-half of its width hardened. If the quench is too deep it will cause too much hard edge and the blade may not have superior flexibility. When the hardening line is too shallow, there won't be enough hard part to give the blade adequate stiffness. One way to get repeatable results with a given width of blade is to place a regulator block at the correct depth under the surface of the oil. The proper depth for the regulator block will be different with each type of steel

and will vary with the quench speed of the oil. It will take some trial and error to work it out.

Hold the blade with tongs to heat it for the edge-quench. As the blade gets close to the hardening temperature, switch to a cool pair of tongs or else cool off the hot pair. When the entire blade or just the edge half gets up to hardening temperature, quench it somewhat point first, then rock it down onto the regulator block. This is necessary so that the full length of the edge is hardened. If all goes well the edge will be hard and the back soft enough to give the blade great strength.

The edge-quench is easiest to get right on wide blades, but with practice it can be used on blades as narrow as 3/4 inches. A blade with a lot of curvature will have to be rocked sufficiently on the regulator block to get the entire cutting edge hardened. After about 15 seconds, the blade can be totally submerged in the oil. The blade should be allowed to cool to the temperature of the oil before removal. Blades should be tempered immediately following hardening. A selectively hardened blade is tempered the same as for a blade that's fully hardened.

The "Goop" Quench

I got started with the goop quench from an old-time blacksmith named Al Bart. I had the good fortune to spend time with Al at the conferences of The Northwest Blacksmith Association. His wisdom came from years of practical experience added onto what had been passed down to him from generations of smiths. He preferred to quench cutting tools in bacon grease. His opinion was that it made them harder than other quenchants. Al figured it was giving a faster quenching action than plain grease because of the salt content. An old book on heat-treating listed the quench speed of a lot of different oils; tallow (animal fat) was listed as the fastest quenchant of the lot.

Cutting tools need to be made as hard as is possible in the quench process and then be tempered back for strength combined with edge-holding ability. When a quenchant cools the blade too slowly, something less than maximum hardness will be achieved and edge-holding ability will not be as good as could have been.

I started my experiments with grease quenching in 1984. I saved up a bunch of fat from the kitchen, put it in an old coffee urn and started using it for quenching. It worked great for getting all types of steel extremely hard.

The heat treat area of the Goddard Smithy. The 10-inch blade is being quenched in the large goop pan. Note the small homemade gas forge above the goop. It's used for forging and heat-treating only. At the left of the goop is the annealing box that contains vermiculite. Under the goop is a pan full of wood ashes that are used for annealing high alloy steel types. The ashes, when preheated, will give a slower cool than the vermiculite.

The old fellow in the coveralls is blacksmith Al Bart. He taught me about using animal fat for quenching edged tools and that led to the goop mixture I now use for almost everything. He was working down a forge weld that joined the two pieces of axle steel to make the hardie-hole bick-anvil.

The forged project blade is ready for the quench.

It was exciting to use because it made a great deal of smoke and fire. It got rancid in time, and it was a problem to keep the neighborhood animals out of it. I reasoned that if it were not so soft it might not get rancid. About that time I bought a huge box of junk candles at a yard sale. I started mixing the grease with an equal part of the junk wax, which was a mix of mostly paraffin with some beeswax in it. I eventually started using the goop for the edge quench and found that it worked very well.

The improved goop didn't get rancid and the animals evidently didn't like the taste of it because they left it alone. It is difficult hauling oil around to demonstrations, so having a quench medium that will not spill works out well. The improved goop stays semi-solid when not in use and is very portable. My traveling outfit is a 2- by 9- by 14-inch cake pan; you can see it in the photo. When traveling, the goop pan sits on end in a 5-gallon bucket. I use a thin piece of plywood for a lid. I surround it with hammers and tongs and off I go for a day of fun. The goop I use in the smithy is in a stainless steel pan from a restaurant hot-table, it's about 4 by 10 by 20 inches. It's just long enough to get a 12-inch blade, full-tang Bowie or camp knife in by going corner to corner.

I improved the goop once more by adding about one quarter by volume of dirty hydraulic fluid and it seems to work even better at getting steel hard. I use it instead of an oil quench for everything except double-edged blades which require tip down, straight-in quench in an oil bath or a preheated goop bath in a deep container like the coffee urn mentioned above.

The heat-treat area for blades over 7 inches is in my outdoor smithy. Nothing fancy, just a tin roof hooked onto the back of my shop. It's open on three sides and I use fans to create positive airflow that comes in one end and out the other. My goop quenchant works out well in the open air because it creates a lot of flame and smoke. I can't recommend using it indoors without some very effective ventilation. There is a lot of smoke and sometimes flames with the larger knives.

Since the first edition of this book I've started experimenting with a pan of goop made by replacing the hydraulic oil with high-temperature, synthetic automatic transmission fluid. It gives the goop a nice reddish color and seems to cut down on the flame and smoke. I harden most small blades (under 8 inches) in the new goop using the one-brick forge in my indoor forge area and I am thinking it is the best goop mix yet.

Hardening The Project Blades

The heat source for the quench party was the forge made from a soft firebrick, a propane torch furnishes the flame. See the chapter "World's Smallest Forge." The

The edge quench in goop.

The appearance of a blade after an edge quench.

goop quench needs no preheating for an edge-quench on small blades like my two project knives. With larger blades I use a scrap piece of heated steel to get a slot of molten goop started. I usually have some small blades to do first and those times it is not necessary to preheat a slot big enough for the knife. The goop burns quite well when overheated, so use caution and keep a lid handy to smother any fire that starts.

The blade is heated slowly and uniformly to the point where it no longer is attracted to a magnet. The temperature is allowed to climb just a little and then the blade is quickly quenched. It is always good to practice getting an even heat on a scrap piece of steel that is close to the size of the finished blade.

The photo shows the forged blade made from the Honda car coil spring as it has just entered the goop. It's getting an edge-quench where just about half the width of the blade is hardened.

The next photo shows the stock-removal blade made from a lawnmower blade. Notice the light-colored appearance of the hardened part of the blade. The violence of the quench causes the scale to explode off of the portion that hardened. Most steel will appear gray when properly quenched; others will appear almost white. This appearance is most always a sign that the blade got hard. Don't assume that a blade got hard; try each and every one with a file to make sure. I use the triangular files used for sharpening saws. When too dull to sharpen saws they are just right for hardness testing and you can usually get them free from a saw shop. Put the edge of the file on the blade and bear down. Nothing but the scale should come off if full hardness was achieved.

Tempering The Blade

The internal structure of steel, when successfully quenched is known as martensite. Martensite is very hard, brittle, highly stressed and unstable. A knife blade in this condition would not survive too long without breaking. The brittle nature of the as-hardened blade has to be softened slightly by tempering. This is accomplished in most carbon and carbon alloy steels used for knife blades by heating the blade to a temperature of between 375 and 450 degrees F and holding it there for a minimum of one hour.

All changes that take place in steel as a result of heating or cooling are a factor of both time and temperature. Tempering is a decomposition of the martensite. A lower temperature for a long time may have the same softening effect as a slightly higher temperature for a short time.

Tempering or drawing to the exact degree of hardness is necessary in order to impart a combination of strength and edge-holding ability. Each steel type has a "working hardness" where it is neither too brittle nor too soft. The steel type, blade length and intended use for the knife should be taken into account in determining the final hardness. The very best steel that has been correctly hardened may fail in service if the temper is not correct.

Triple Tempering

Tempering should be done three times for at least one hour. Austenite that did not transform in the quenching process can form untempered martensite while cooling from the tempering cycle. The tempering process not only softens the steel to a usable degree but it can transform retained austenite. The second and third tempers are necessary to soften any newly formed martensite. Blades should be allowed to cool to room temperature between temper cycles.

Another reason for triple tempering is that the heat may not be even over the length of the blade when using a tempering gizmo, torch, or whatever. The second and third temper cycles will help to create a more uniform final hardness. The additional time at temperature will help the tempering process to be complete.

The Working Hardness

The proper hardness for a blade is somewhat of a balancing act. The harder a blade is with simple steels like 1084, 1095 and 5160, the more abrasive-resistant it will be. When it applies to knife blades, abrasive-resistance is the same as edge-holding ability. However, if the blade is too hard it will chip or break in use. When too soft it will not hold an edge. The working hardness is the maximum hardness where the blade will still have adequate strength for its intended purpose. This hardness is best worked out through a testing procedure and not left to an educated guess.

For those of us who heat-treat our own blades it is imperative to have some type of test procedure to determine if what we are turning out will hold up against the best. A blade needs to be compared to a blade of known value in order to determine the worth of any heat treating procedure.

Stock-removal makers using proven steels and a reputable heat treater can have pretty good faith in their blades. Paul Bos, a heat treater specializing in knife blades for many years does my stainless steel blades. I have the ultimate amount of confidence in his work and can sell my stainless steel knives knowing that they will meet the full potential of the steel type.

A Toaster Oven For Tempering

A toaster-oven in the knife shop will help keep peace in the family. I tempered knives in the kitchen oven for almost 20 years. It was hard to get all the oil off of the blades and there was usually some smell of smoke in the house during tempering. I finally figured out I could do it in the shop with a toaster oven. The first one I had cost

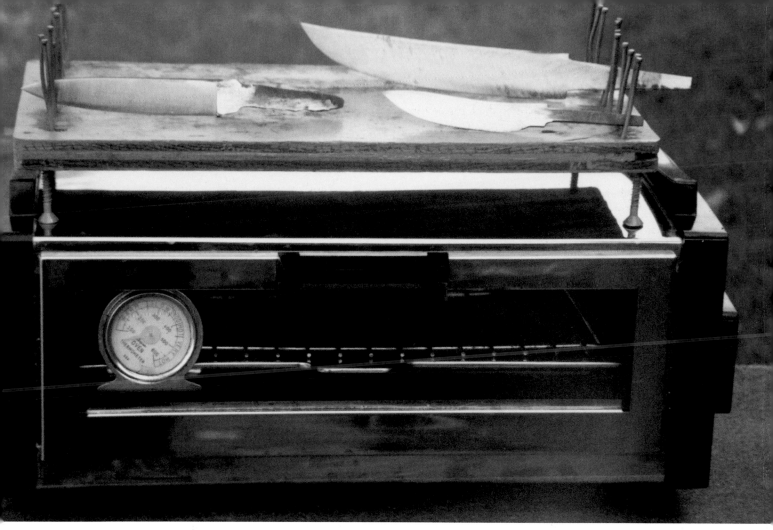

The $50 Knife Shop toaster oven. Note the rack on top that holds the blades between temper cycles. It's just a piece of plywood on legs made of small bolts, nails are driven in to support the blades while cooling.

35 cents at an as-is thrift store. All it needed was a rack and a knob for the heat control. In order to remain true to the cheap-tool philosophy of *The $50 Knife Shop* series, I recently bought a toaster oven at a thrift store for $2. See the photo. I used it to temper the two knives I am working on in this series.

The Soft Back Draw

The soft back draw was the only way it was being done before the edge quench came along about 1985. We did it with an oxygen/acetylene torch. Propane is not hot enough and the heat applied to the back portion of the blade travels down the blade and softens the edge too much before the back gets up to the necessary temperature. That was the way I learned and here is how we did it. The blade was first fully hardened and then cleaned down to bare metal. An oxygen/acetylene torch with a #00 or smaller tip was cranked up so it was running very hot. The tip of the blue cone in the flame was applied to the back of the hardened knife. Almost immediately a blue color would

show and it was necessary to start moving the torch down the spine of the blade.

The object was to get a nice even blue line full length down the back of the blade. If the torch tip was moved too slowly the heat would move down too close to the edge. When this happened there would be an excess of softening of the blade it would have to be annealed and rehardened. It took a lot of practice to get good at it. I still teach the soft back draw because it is a good way to improve the strength of a finished knife blade that had been fully hardened. It is added insurance for an edge-quenched blade that appears to have too much hard edge. After using both methods and getting good test results I switched to the edge quench because, once worked out, it's easier to get the correct degree of stiffness in a blade.

The Tempering Gizmo

It is nearly impossible to draw the temper on a blade in a gas forge, the reason is a gas forge will not run at the low temperature required. (375 to 500 degrees F).

Soft Back Draw

#1

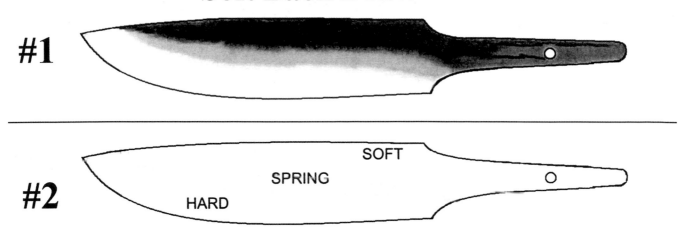

#2

SOFT

SPRING

HARD

Edge Quenched

Blade #1 shows the relationship and proportion of the color bands visible from the soft-back draw. Blade #2 shows the approximate relationship of hard, springy and soft from the edge quench. Blade #2 also shows the approximate line that the blade is inserted into the oil when edge-quenched. Both methods can be adjusted to give the same amount of hard edge. The edge-quenched blades will usually show more flexibility before the edge cracks for two reasons. First is because the width of the hard edge is narrower, at least the way I do it, and second, because the back is usually softer.

COLOR	APPROXIMATE TEMPERATURE
YELLOW	420 F
STRAW	450 F
BROWN	480 F
PURPLE	550 F
DARK BLUE	590 F
GREENISH BLUE	630 F

A blade with a soft back temper will show the color rainbow similar to the one in the photo. The color is the result of an oxide layer formed by the heat and is a true indication of the temperature reached in the steel. Be aware that the same temperature will cause different colors on the surface of steel types of differing alloy content. Practice on a junk blade until you get the process consistent enough to do it on a finished blade.

When steel is heated to approximately 400 to 450 degrees F a layer of oxide, which appears as a straw color, forms on the surface. As the temperature increases the oxide color changes, and is a fairly accurate way to judge the temperature of the steel. When three different steel types are tempered at the same time and same temperature they will each show a slightly different color. The alloy content of the steel causes the color difference.

The tempering gizmo with a blade in it.

I have experimented with tempering many different ways and the easiest way to get an even temper is to use an electric oven. The one in your kitchen will do, or you can use a toaster oven from a thrift store. The disadvantage of an even temper is that the blade does not have all the flexible strength that is possible when the back has been softened.

In an attempt to soften the back on a fully hardened blade I experimented with resting the back of the blade on a hot piece of steel or copper. It was possible to get an even temper but I couldn't get the back much softer than the edge. Tempering on a heated steel plate brings the color down too slowly. To soften the back, the heat has to be high and localized at the spine of the blade. The blade back must reach a full blue in order to give the blade great flexible strength. The difficult part is to get the blue temper color on the back of the blade without overheating the edge.

What I needed was a tempering gizmo that could be heated in the one-brick forge. See the photo. I made it out of copper and stainless steel scrap. The copper sides are 3/8-inch thick, 7/8-inch wide and about 4 inches long. The jig is riveted together with stainless pins made of TIG wire. The sides could be made of common steel or brass. Steel will scale away whereas copper or brass will last longer. The whole jig could be made of stainless steel if it is available. The gap where the blade back is heated is 1/4-inch wide, but could be as narrow as your thickest knife blade. The spacer bar/handle piece was a scrap of 304 stainless that just happened to be wider on one end. I shaped the wide end into a grip surface for my forge-use ViseGrip® pliers and then gave it a half turn

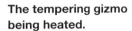
The tempering gizmo being heated.

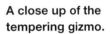
A close up of the tempering gizmo.

so it will sit flat. See the photo. Recently I added a separate removable copper bar that is approximately 1/4-inch by 1/4-inch. It is necessary to have it in place when doing really narrow blades. Without the spacer bar they drop too far down into the jig and then it is more difficult to get the back soft before the edge overheats.

The blade to be tempered should be finished down to bare and clean metal. That means no buffing compound or fingerprints. Anything greasy will throw the temper colors off and/or make them hard to keep even. The jig is heated to a red/orange color in the one-brick forge and then taken out and rested on top of the forge. The torch is shut down at that time. The blade is then lowered back down into the gap and slowly worked back and forth to get an even color. The ricasso is given the most attention because it will take more heat to get tempered than the tip. The tip will come along without giving it much attention. Have a shallow pan handy with about 1/2 an inch of water in it. If the temper color at the edge gets past light brown, the edge should be cooled in the water. Put it in a little at a time in order to reduce the shock of sudden cooling.

The soft back temper is correct when the back 1/3 of the blade shows a good blue color and the color at the edge has not gone past brown. Lightly sand the blade to remove the color and repeat the process two more times.

Hardened and Tempered, What Next?

It would be wonderful if there was a universal formula for hardening and tempering that could be used for the first time and the results would be a perfectly usable knife blade. It just doesn't work that way in real life for most of us. That's because of the many variables that influence the results. It is unlikely that the results from hardening and tempering the first few blades of a specific steel type will be exactly right. Just for fun, let's pretend the heat-treatment did come out perfectly; but how do we know that unless some type of comparison is made with a blade of known value? My opinion is that complete and total confidence in one's product can only result as the product of some type of testing program.

A knife blade can be either too hard or too soft. It's not hard to figure; too hard and it will chip or break. When too soft, it won't stay sharp, or in the case of a large knife, it could be bent during normal use. It's a fine line between the extremes where a specific type of steel is the exact hardness where it will hold up in normal use. That's why the blade should be tested for toughness after it is tempered and before the handle is put on. See the brass rod test below.

Cutting on almost anything will dull a blade enough to get an idea of what it will do when compared to a blade

Mike Draper has passed the 90-degree flex test as part of the Journeyman Smith requirements for the American Bladesmith Society. Eye protection is always worn for the flex test; this picture was posed after the test was completed. (The Master Smith can't control the test and look through a camera lens at the same time.)

of known value. James Black, legendary maker of Jim Bowie knives, was supposed to have tested his knives by whittling hickory for an hour. That's according to Governor Jones in Raymond Thorp's book Bowie Knife. Black would discard any knife that would not shave hair from his arm after the test. Now, that's tough testing!

The Brass Rod Test

Those doing their own heat-treating should learn this test even if they do no other testing. The Brass Rod Test was shown to me 45 years ago by a blacksmith who made knives in the 1920s and 1930s. I started using it in about 1975 and I have found it to be a quick and accurate judgment of edge strength. This test is performed on a finished blade that does not have a handle attached. Once the handle is in place any necessary adjustments to the heat treat can not be done. It is a test of the heat-treating more than it is of the steel type. It is simple to perform and works for all types of steel. The test is intended for fairly thin working type hunting knife blades. A thick blade with a heavy edge cannot be evaluated with this test. Find yourself a scrap of wood with a big knot in it and chop through it with your thick-bladed camp knife, if it doesn't hold up to that it shouldn't be sold as a camp knife.

Clamp a 1/4-inch diameter brass rod horizontally in a vise with the top half above the jaws. Lay the edge on the brass rod at the same angle used for sharpening (approximately 15 degrees). Apply enough pressure so that you can see the edge deflect from the pressure on the rod. When tested on a scale the pressure works out to 30 to 35 pounds. Have a good light source behind the vise so that you can see the deflection.

If the edge chips out with moderate pressure on the rod, the edge will most likely chip out in use. If the edge stays bent over in the deflected area, it will bend in use and be too soft to hold an edge. When the deflected edge springs back straight the temper is correct. If the edge chips the tempering temperature should be increased 25 degrees and the temper repeated for 90 minutes. Keep this up until the edge passes the test. If the edge stayed deflected it needs to be annealed, then hardened and tempered at a lower temperature.

When demonstrating at knife shows it isn't feasible to take a vise along so I wanted to have the brass rod test in a portable form. I used super glue to attach a piece of brass rod to a piece of hardwood. It can then be rested on any sturdy surface to perform the test. See the photo.

The brass rod test setup.

Cutting Rope To Test Edge-Holding Ability

Years ago I tried to test the edge-holding ability of knives by cutting cardboard. The amount of time and large amount of cardboard it took to dull a blade made it impractical. When I started cutting rope I discovered that it dulled a blade quickly and uniformly. I use 1/2-inch diameter rope or the single strands unraveled out of 1-inch or larger rope. Comparisons need to be with knives of the same general length, thickness and general cross section at the edge. Sharpening needs to be uniform between test blades. Slicing cuts are made until the edge loses its bite in the rope. I like to cut and sharpen three times and average the results. The comparison tests with the knife of known value should be done on the same day with the same rope. The important thing is to make some type of comparison. Other test materials could be rolled up newspaper, sections out of a phone book or magazine, rubber strips or leather. All of these things will work for cutting tests but some of them can get expensive and tiring. Slicing on rope gets the test over in a reasonable amount of time.

The $50 Knife Shop series is about how to make knives with very simple equipment. Although the equipment is cheap a high-quality knife can be made. The time spent with some basic test procedures will not only be a good investment in your knowledge base but will make the subsequent finishing details all the more meaningful. You'll have a total package that you can be proud of and also be confident that it will perform well in use.

Something Went Wrong

Here is a hypothetical example: A piece of the finest grade of steel was forged on the "ultimate anvil." A very special "magic" hammer was used throughout the forging. The latest in computer-controlled electric furnaces was used for thermal cycles after the forging. Digital read-outs monitored the progress. The latest variable-speed "Mark XIV" belt grinder was used to clean up the blade. The computer-controlled vacuum furnace was used for the hardening and tempering. The heat-treated blade was then tested for hardness with a Rockwell test machine that had recently been calibrated by the Bureau of Standards. The knife was then finished and delivered to the customer. After using it a while, the customer returned it to the maker with a complaint about poor cutting ability. A committee of experts was called in to check the blade. The committee's findings were that the blade was too thick at the edge. The maker thinned it down and returned it to the customer. Shortly thereafter, the customer complained about chipping at the edge. Once more the knife was returned and checked by the committee. This time the determination was that the blade was too hard for its intended purpose. Regardless of the knifemaker's equipment and method of shaping the blade, the total package had not been attained. Instead of buying more equipment, the hypothetical maker should have invested some of his time in testing his knives.

CHAPTER 5

PRIMITIVE KNIFEMAKING

The philosophy of primitive knifemaking revolves around simplicity and economy of materials and equipment. Doesn't that sound a lot like *The $50 Knife Shop*? Using recycled materials and being energy efficient is emphasized and part of that is learning how to do it without using electricity. Others and myself find it fun and challenging to see what can be made with less instead of more. An example would be to figure out how to make knives without a grinder instead of buying a more powerful grinder.

The kit knife made by the Neo Tribal Bladesmiths. I finished mine with a rawhide wrap.

The washtub charcoal forge.

Tai Goo's tribal forge area.

I call it the hand-crank shop. It's the modified table-top forge outfit with the addition of a hand-crank grinder and drill press. I'm not going to let a power shortage bother me.

A large part of what the handmade knife world is about is not based on reality. Knife shows and magazines are full of knives that originated on a sketchpad or drawing board. Often there was no evolutionary process that brought them to where they are. These knives may find acceptance in the make-believe marketplace but they would have a hard time surviving in real-life applications.

From my point of view, primitive-style knives are based on reality and made to do work. They have a legitimate ancestry and if they could talk, they would tell us where they came from. A primitive-style knife would rather be at work than resting on a satin pillow in a knife collection.

My Version Of Primitive Knifemaking

It wasn't very long after I got seriously into forging that I started a series that I called tribal knives. The purpose was to finish knives that had the appearance of

being old. I've never done replicas of old knives; I'd rather do my version of them. I wanted them to look somewhat earthy, without being too crude, but at the same time have good workmanship.

My main inspiration was an African throwing knife that had somewhat of a hook or hatchet type blade. The blade was one of the most expertly forged edged tools that I had ever seen. It was completely shaped with a hammer; only the edge portion was finished with what appeared to be a very fine stone. There was no stock removal as we think of it.

For myself, primitive knifemaking has to do with my attitude towards the tools, materials and finished product. For starters, if I buy new steel it's not remotely primitive enough. An important part of being "Tribal" is to learn to test junkyard materials, then figure out how to work them and determine what they are good for. It's better to learn how to work junk steel than to mess up new steel with bad heat-treating. There are already too many knives being made that have poorly heat treated blades.

I enjoy the challenge of eliminating all tools that are not absolutely necessary. I develop a level of intimacy with my primitive knives that doesn't exist with my "modern-made" knives. Forging to the finished shape and hand finishing is as up close and personal as it can get. I don't find that same connection when I grind a blade to shape; stock removal is a more distant process.

The forged knife for *the $50 Knife Shop* series was made without electricity and is about as primitive as it gets. I can't imagine that I'd ever want to work completely without electricity but I know that I could if I had to. I'm fascinated enough with the primitive methods that I can see it always being part of my work.

The primitive method forces the smith to be very careful with the finished forging. If the forged blade is not close to the final shape, smooth and flat, there is so much material to remove that it becomes nearly impossible to finish the blade with files and hand stones. It becomes a challenge to see how close to the finished shape a blade can be forged. I didn't realize how sloppy my forging was until I started trying to finish blades by hand. I found myself going back to the forge several times to make the edge thinner or to get out a twist, lump or hammer mark.

The Neo-Tribal Metalsmiths

An organization known as The Neo-Tribal Metalsmiths existed for about five years. Some people say that it started in Tai Goo's backyard, in 1995. Tai doesn't think so. Although the Neo-Tribal Metalsmiths no longer exists as an organization, the tribal philosophy is alive and growing.

"All I did was recognize it, and then tried to get others to appreciate it," says Goo. Tai believes that the tribal way is really the standard way in most other parts of the world and that for some reason we have become alienated from the ancestral metalsmiths by modern Western culture.

Tim Lively put it like this, "Looking to history rather than new technology to resolve problems arising from the enjoyable pastime of trying to re-create traditional tools and weapons, we emphasize the use of primitive tools and techniques. We allow limited use of modern tools only to help you through the process until the simpler more primitive way can be rediscovered. We strive to bring back the simplicity and high quality of the ancient masters. Such as hand/eye coordination, hand tools, and natural materials. Minimalism. We also take full advantage of life in the throw-away society. We recycle the abundant scrap and turn it into high quality art. We want to remember how great, great grandpa did it."

A Real Tribal Knife

This primitive knife wasn't too highly thought of by the seller at a knife show. It was in a box of junk knives that were all priced at $2. This knife told quite a story, much more than the stainless steel hunting knife on the next table. Inspection showed that the knife blade was made by forge welding smaller pieces of scrap together. Note the visible weld joints and the welding flaw at the tip. I don't think it is unreasonable to believe that this blade contained all the steel that the smith had on hand at the time. The tang is minimal in order to save on material. Close inspection shows that a piece of iron was forge welded to the steel blade to form the tang. It was done that

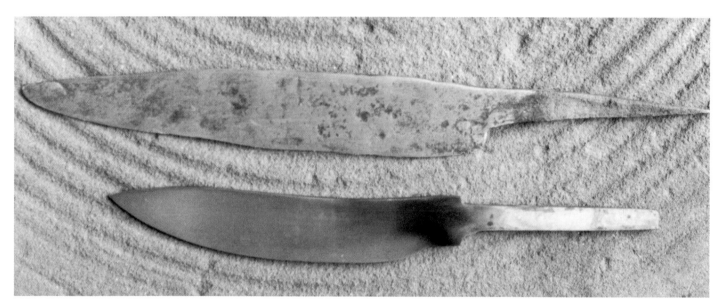

The tribal knife blade showing the tang detail. The blade at the bottom was the forged project for The $50 Knife Shop project. It qualifies as tribal because no electricity or power tools were used to make it. The heat color is the result of hot fitting the tang in to the handle.

A genuine tribal knife.

This photo shows the tabletop forge from the back side, note how the vise is set up. I'm holding the blade between a fire brick and the fire chamber to heat for the quench. Tempering was carefully done the same way. Gene Chapman is at the right trying to catch up with me.

way to save on the precious commodity known as steel.

This knife has an iron ferrule to strengthen the handle while in use. It might have prevented the handle from splitting apart when the tang was driven into the handle material. The tang was fitted into the tree-branch handle by burning it in. The split in the handle looks more like it dried out too fast rather than being damaged by hard use.

This is the simplest type of construction I can imagine. This type of knife is common in all parts of the world and has been since the first metal knife blades were put in

handles. The blade shape would do many things well. I've seen pictures and documentary movies of larger, similar knives being used to dress game in Africa.

Tabletop Forging

The idea of tabletop forging started when I put together a portable forging outfit for use at demonstrations. I used a Black & Decker WorkMate for a base and everything but the anvil fits on it. I bolted a vise to a 2 by 6 board and used the clamp part of the WorkMate to hold it in place. The vise holder had a leg that went to the ground to stabilize it.

I hauled that portable shop around in a 1976 Honda station wagon and must have gone traveling with it a dozen times. I had a lot of fun with it but everything was a lot larger than it really needed to be. The pictures were taken in Washington State at a Northwest Safari Cutlery Rendezvous. I'm in the middle of a speed-forging contest with Gene Chapman.

The rules for the contest were pretty simple. The participants started out with a hot forge and a cold piece of steel. The blade had to be forged, hardened, tempered and sharpened. The first one to shave hair with a finished blade was the winner. My experience with primitive methods

The early edition of the tabletop forging setup.

The one-brick forge is set up on the tabletop. Note the tempering gizmo with a blade in place. A favorite hammer, ViseGrip® pliers and hay rake material are on top of the $15 anvil.

paid off because I won the event two years in row.

The finished blades from this contest were not subjected to all the correct heat-treating procedures that they should have been. Nevertheless, all those who participated learned a lot. The legal starting material could be a rectangle so I used a piece of hay rake tooth that had been previously forged into a bar about 3/4 inch by 1/4 inch. I quickly forged a 3- inch blade as close as I could to shape. Steel is more easily filed when hot so I went to work on it with a file as it was still cooling. I then smoothed it up very roughly and quickly with a hand stone. Once it was reheated I quenched it and did a quick temper. I then sharpened it and shaved some hair off my arm. I won the contest in 1995 with an elapsed time of 17 minutes and 41 seconds. The blade wasn't pretty and it didn't have a handle but it did what a knife was supposed to do.

The one-brick forge opens up forging to anyone who has the space that a small table occupies. A table isn't the best support for a makeshift anvil from the scrap yard, but it can be made to work if there is nothing else available. The anvil will work best on a table if it is positioned directly over a leg, otherwise a piece of 4-by-4 fence post could be wedged between the bottom of the table and the floor.

I assembled my tabletop forge area on a Black and Decker WorkMate #88 that I got at a yard sale. The anvil is a 55-pound rectangle of steel that cost me $12 at the scrap yard. I set up the one-brick forge directly behind the anvil and I was ready to go. I forged a small blade from a hay rake tooth and it went pretty smoothly. The anvil was noisy and bounced around a little bit so I clamped it to the table and it worked a lot better.

In order to make it a true primitive knife the blade should be finished without electricity using files and stones. The blade will be heated for the quench process in the one-brick forge or other primitive heat source. The one-brick tempering jig will be used for getting the hardness just right. I've got a nice branch from the dogwood tree in my front yard that will furnish the handle material. I'll use a copper ferrule to wedge the blade into the handle. All operations will be done on the tabletop.

The forge and all necessary tools except the anvil can be carried in a couple of five-gallon buckets. I've got the table-top forge in its portable version worked out really well and travel with it often.

See the photo for the 2005 version of the table-top forge outfit.

How To Make A Wavy Blade Dagger

The most famous wavy-blade dagger would be the Kris, mystic weapon of Malaysia and Indonesia. This type blade is sometimes called a flaming blade. Daggers and swords with flaming blades were made in Europe over a long period of time

I wanted to do a wavy blade dagger as part of my tribal series of knives but when I tried to find out the procedure for forging one I came up dry. No one in the knife world could give me a clue. Finally, my bladesmith friend Art Swyhart sent me a video clip of a kids program called "Paco's Fun House". The video showed a smith from Malaysia making a traditional wavy-blade dagger (Kris). The proper phonetic pronunciation is "Kress".

The smith on the video used a charcoal fire to weld up a billet of what looked like a mixture of railroad spikes and some other steel. The billet was forged into a tapered pre-form. The smith then put the waves in using a bottom tool that looked like it may have been the head of a huge sledgehammer. Once the waves were in he went to work forging the bevels. The native bladesmith with the primitive tools made it all look very easy. By the time I had watched the video half a dozen times I was ready to attempt forging a wavy-blade dagger.

Procedure For Forging a Wavy Blade Dagger

The way I teach forging is that all blades start with a specific pre-form. The steel bar is forged to a certain shape (a pre-form) so that it will have the correct shape and width once the hammer blows spread the edge or edges out. When a pre-form is not made prior to forging the bevels there can be a problem getting the blade shape correct. When the bevel is forged into a single edged blade the tip always curves up and more often than not there will be too much belly in the edge.

Starting with the correct pre-form helps combat the excess curvature. Learning the proper shape and size of a pre-form for each different blade shape is something that is learned primarily by experience. A general rule is that the finished blade will be somewhere in the neighborhood of 30 to 50 percent wider than the pre-form. Forging a specific shape is especially critical for the tribal bladesmith when all the finishing is to be done by hand with files or stones.

Wavy-blade dagger forged from 1095 flat bar stock. There was no stock removal except for the sharpening bevel. The guard was forged to shape and hot fitted to the tang. Elk antler furnished the handle that has a copper pommel cap. The maple sheath has a copper throat.

Forging a double-edged blade has some unique problems associated with it.

How much narrower should the pre-form be from the finished profile? Trial and error rules here, the exact width of the pre-form will depend somewhat on the thickness of the bar stock and how thin it is forged at the edge.

Double-edged blades are difficult to hold on the anvil at the correct angle to get the bevels even.

If the blade is not kept flat on the anvil the hammer causes a bending blow that twists the blade.

The final problem is keeping the forging even on all four surfaces of the blade in order for the finished blade to be symmetrical. Whenever a dagger blade takes on a curve in one direction, it is the result of uneven forging. When the bevels are evened up, the tip should be back on the centerline.

The pre-form is having waves formed with a top and bottom tool. Note the thickening at the bottom of the waves, it is important to keep this material pushed back into the pre-form as work progresses. The top tool is a reworked ball peen hammer, the bottom tool is a ship's maul that has the edges of the eye well rounded.

A first project should be made from 1/4-inch by 1-inch bar stock and the blade will be 8 inches long. Start by forging a dagger pre-form that is 70 percent of the width that the finished wavy blade should be. Some, but not too much, distal taper should be forged into the pre-form. If this is not done the dagger point may be wider than was expected. Don't try to forge any bevels just yet, that will all be done with a specially shaped ball-end hammer. The pre-form has to be symmetrical or else the finished piece won't be. If necessary file or grind it to a symmetrical shape before forging the waves in.

Making Waves

A top tool and bottom a tool are both required to make the waves. The shape of the bottom tool sets up the distance between the waves. I'm told that there is some significance associated with the number of waves in the traditional Kris blade. For myself, it's left up to chance as

to how many waves work out for the length of the blade. I've adopted a style that makes a tighter wave than is found on most wavy-blade daggers. With good control a fuller shaped top tool can be used to push the dagger form down into the bottom tool. I prefer to have a striker so that I can control both the blade and top tool. While putting the waves in, the blade will curve first one way and then the other but it should come out even in the end. It is important to keep the thickness even so some flattening and adjusting will need to be done during the wave-making process.

Forging Dagger Bevels

Once the waves are complete the bevels can be forged. In order to get down into the bottom of the waves I use a hammer that was made by grinding the hammer end of a standard ball-peen into a large ball. This makes a strike pattern on the steel that is similar to that seen on many

The relationship of the tools for making a wave.

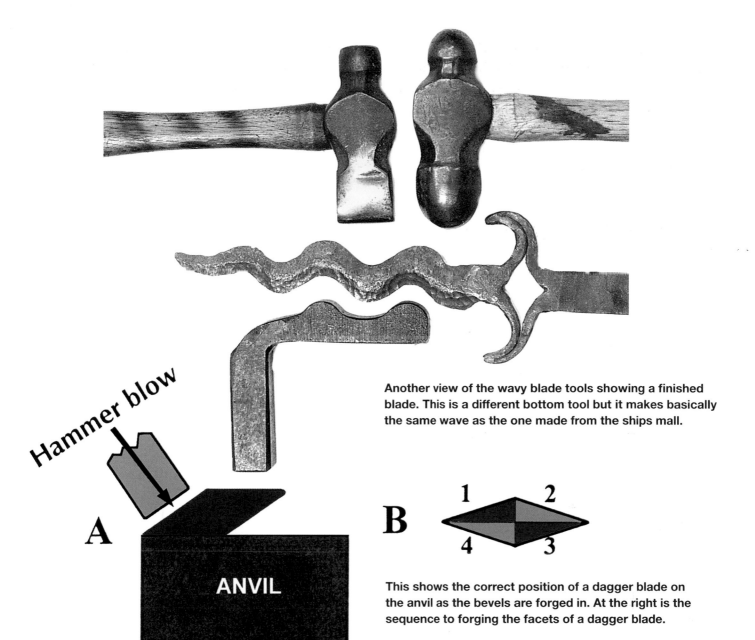

A Hammer blow

ANVIL

Another view of the wavy blade tools showing a finished blade. This is a different bottom tool but it makes basically the same wave as the one made from the ships mall.

B

This shows the correct position of a dagger blade on the anvil as the bevels are forged in. At the right is the sequence to forging the facets of a dagger blade.

African blades that are totally forged to shape. The bottom of a wave has to sit exactly on the edge of the anvil or a bending blow will result. Sometimes the corner of the flat face of the anvil will work just fine; other waves require a rounded edge under the blade.

If you look at finished dagger blade from the end you will see four facets. They are numbered 1, 2, 3, and 4 in a clockwise direction. See the drawing. I adopted a style where the bevel is forged into one side of each edge; the African knife that inspired my tribal series was forged that way. For example, all the hammer blows to put the taper in would be on 1 and 3. It takes a lot of hammering to do it this way but the results are worth the effort. The tribal dagger with no stock removal will be forged very close to the final thickness at the edge.

For a more symmetrical cross section, the bevel-forging blows would be equally spaced between the four facets. Start the forging by working a bevel on the surface that will become facet 1 of the blade. It is of the utmost importance to not make any hammer blows past the centerline. As you work along the edge the forged portion will belly out from the opposite edge. Don't worry, it will straighten itself out with the next forging. Forge the same amount of bevel into facet 3. If you forged both edges equally the shape will be symmetrical.

Now go to facet 2, and finally 4. By alternating the facets it is easier to keep everything even. Keep working around the blade in this manner, all the time being aware of where the anvil is under the blade. If you don't keep the anvil under the flat side of the blade you will be putting

A wavy-blade dagger in wire damascus with a handle made from the tip of a walrus tusk. Making this type knife is what I call having fun.

kinks and bends in the blade and that will make the forging harder.

It is easy to tell if you are forging everything equally, as you look at the profile it will be symmetrical, and when you look at it from the point end you will see a diamond shape. Forge and look, forge and look. This is a difficult blade to forge so take it slow and easy. If you are going to finish-grind the blade, take the bevels down to a flat where the edges meet that is approximately 1/16-inch thick. You will need this much material in order to clean up the blade prior to heat-treating. If you forge the bevels too thin at the edge, a dagger that uses grinding to finish it can get too narrow really quickly.

I enjoy making wavy-blade daggers because it is a challenge and not something that too many others are doing.

The Wedge Power Primitive Vise

Here is a picture of my primitive vise, blade and knife holder. I got the idea from the blade holders the Japanese and other South-Seas bladesmiths use. It is more than adequate to hold a blade on a support board for drawfiling or hand stoning. The board is maple scrap from a cabinet shop. The U-bolt was from a junk box at a yard sale. The wedges are made from lilac that grew in my yard. This fixture has excellent gripping power on whatever is wedged into it. I made an insert that allows me to wedge a handle piece in place vertically and horizontally at the same time. I use a wedge faced with leather when holding wood handle material.

I use what I call a knife board to support the blade for drawfiling and hand sanding. These knife boards are the approximate shape of the blade and are adjusted so that they always overhang the knife tip by just a little. The photo shows the wedge power vise holding a knife board with blade in place.

It is unsafe to work on unsupported blades. One misstep when a blade is hanging out of a vise can lead to a serious injury. Using a knife board is much safer and more pressure with better control can applied when the blade is supported. A collision with the point of an unsupported blade could be deadly so it's not worth taking a chance by working on an unprotected blade sticking out of a vise.

The $10 Knife Shop

Many years ago a friend showed me a handmade watch chain that was made of little folding knives. If my memory

The wedge power primitive vise.

serves me right there were eight or more of the single blade folding knives. Each was joined to the other by a handmade chain link. They were about an inch long, with nickel silver liners and bolsters with red plastic handles. The only tool used was a fingernail file. Material for the little knives came from table knives and the handle material from toothbrushes. An inmate made them in prison as a gift for a lady who had befriended him. Seeing work like this left a definite impression on me. It shows patience, skill and determination to get the job done with the only tool that was available.

Miniature knives and knives as jewelry have been made for thousands of years. The nice thing about the little knives is that they can be made with minimal equipment. The smaller a knife blade is, the harder it is to use power equipment to shape it. This becomes the territory where files and hand work rule supreme. The miniature knives I make are mostly made with the simplest of hand tools. A jeweler's saw, some files, a motor-tool, sandpaper and some scrap materials are pretty much enough to do the job.

While on a trip to Idaho to spend Independence Day with relatives I hatched the idea to see if I could put together a set of tools to make a small, simple knife and keep the investment under $10. It took a part of two different days looking for bargain tools but I had everything I needed and hadn't gone over my $10 goal. I haven't had time to complete a project with the tools but proved my point that a $10 Knife Shop is possible.

The tools gathered for the $10 Knife Shop Project. (that's right, $10. A future project.)

CHAPTER 6

DAMASCUS STEEL

What Is Damascus Steel?

Damascus steel was easy to define back in 1973 when Bill Moran first laid out his pattern-welded blades at the Knifemakers Guild Show. It's not so easy these days. At one time I made a list of damascus types that had 18 names on it. Electrical discharge machining, powder filled patterns, layers made of powder metallurgy steel — there is no limit. The knife is no longer just a cutting tool or weapon, it has become a "canvas" where makers of damascus steel can express their art.

Group of damascus knives made by the author for a knife show in the early 1990s.

Mosaic damascus tile made by Ed Schempp.

A look into the mouth of the "Dragon."

Perhaps the future will see the development of an art form where patterned steel is simply hung on the wall or made into sculptural pieces. A customer once asked me to make up sample pieces of all the different patterns and types of damascus steel. It would have been a collection to admire and study but I never found time to do it. Perhaps bladesmiths should start making up standard size sample pieces to sell to collectors; 1 inch by 2 inches would be a nice size.

I tried to sell some small wire damascus sculptural pieces but no one took them seriously enough to make a purchase. I like to think it was because I'm not an artist with papers hanging on the wall that say so. (I suppose it might be possible that my attempts were not actually artistic enough to attract a buyer.)

The following information will not make anyone a master at welding damascus steel but it should make the road a little easier to travel. The general principles apply to all types of forge-welded damascus. The chapter that follows will give more detail on my specialty in damascus steel and that's the type made out of wire rope.

Forge Welding

Forge welding is an ancient process that was essential to all iron and steel working trades. When steel and iron are heated above the upper critical temperature it is possible for them to be joined together by the process we call forge welding. As iron and steel are heated the atoms move faster and faster until they reach a point where they interchange with the atoms of an adjacent and compatible material. The difficulty with this simple-sounding process is that for it to be successful there can be no oxygen or insoluble scale present. (Scale is a form of iron oxide formed when the carbon burns out of sufficiently hot steel.)

The ancient smiths took small pieces of steel and iron and forge welded them together to make a larger piece of material. As an example, forge welding was essential in order to get pieces of material large enough to make a sword. Apprentices learned to weld by keeping all the scraps of iron welded together so it would be ready for whatever was needed. Horseshoes were traditionally made out of welded up bars of iron scrap.

Steel was scarce, so most cutting tools were made with an iron body with steel welded on at the edge. It probably didn't take long for those ancient workmen to determine that working up layers of iron and steel together would make superior material. The modern bladesmith utilizes forge welding as a method of creating many different types of patterned steel.

The author shown welding a billet of motorcycle chain under a Beaudry power hammer. This hammer is in the shop of Joe Elliot in Redmond, Oregon. The event was a workshop sponsored by The North West Blacksmith Association.

This pattern-welded billet has been tripled prior to the second welding heat.

Forge welding is simple once it's been done for a while, yet the factors involved can be complex and confusing. There is a certain instinct that develops as experience is gained. It finally comes to a point that it "feels right" when the atmosphere and heat are correct for welding.

Atmosphere

There are three types of flames; neutral, oxidizing, and reducing or carbonizing. The neutral flame is chemically neutral; it has neither an excess of gas or oxygen. The oxidizing flame has an excess of oxygen, and is easy to identify by the large amount of scale being formed as the hot steel oxidizes. The reducing or carbonizing flame is slightly rich with gas. This is the flame necessary for good forge welding.

I adjust my propane welding furnace until I have a moderate flame coming out of the front. To check the atmosphere I place a piece of steel in the furnace and observe the surface as it comes up to the temperature of the liner. It is an oxidizing atmosphere if there is a lot of scale and dirty-looking junk forming on the surface of the steel. All gas forge/furnaces are a little different so the adjustments have to be worked with to get the best results. Once scale has formed on a piece of steel, it should be wire brushed or scraped to remove the scale before returning it to the furnace. The scale comes off easily at around 1,400 degrees F.

When the billet in the furnace looks wet and runny the atmosphere is reducing. The surface of the billet will look like a yellow ice cube that's melting. Welding will be possible at lower temperatures with a reducing atmosphere. Increasing the gas at this point will cause the atmosphere to become too rich and the steel will start to form scale. The scale that forms on steel is insoluble at the low end of the welding temperature. When heated close to the melting point the scale will become more soluble but this temperature is not easily reached in most gas forges. A coal fire will easily get hot enough to melt the scale and the billet too if care is not taken. Working close to the melting temperature will give good welds but is not good for the quality of the finished blade. It's best to learn how to get a reducing atmosphere and weld at a lower temperature.

Flaws

I've been making damascus for 22 years and certainly don't have it reduced to a science just yet. Finding a flaw in a blade will make me want to sit down and cry. My percentage of flaws is very small today but they still do happen and it's a costly occurrence. Most of mine can be traced to not getting the materials all pushed together at the welding heat. My furnace runs very consistently but if the materials don't contact each other at the welding heat there will be a flaw. Wire damascus billets should be worked into a square or rectangle on the first heat, the next heat should be used to forge the billet from corner to corner, back into a square. This helps the material in the comers get pushed against the rest of the material in the billet.

Soak Time

Soaking is holding the billet at the welding heat for an extended period of time. It's a good idea to increase the soak time whenever flaws are occurring. It takes a couple of minutes for the action of the molten borax to dissolve any scale that's on or in the billet. Soaking the billet for up to five minutes will give added insurance against flaws. There will be more decarburization of the billet and more diffusion of carbon between the layers but the welds will be better. It comes down to working a balance between what it takes to get good welds and having enough carbon left to make a serviceable blade.

Flux

The only flux I use is anhydrous borax. There are some that work with household borax but I never got the good results with it that I do with anhydrous. The flux acts to protect the surface of the steel from forming scale. If and when scale forms the borax acts on and reacts with the scale, lowering the melting point of the scale. This allows welds to be made at a lower temperature than would be possible without the borax acting as a flux. The steel should be fluxed on the rising heat at around 1,300 degrees F. At this temperature the scale has not yet had a chance to form.

The Welding Temperature

The exact welding temperature isn't always easy to judge. Sometimes I think I have it but the steel does not stick together. I believe it varies with the humidity, atmospheric temperature, and the adjustment of the furnace. I remember a very wet and windy day in March, I was welding in a brick box furnace I made. The wind was blowing a fine mist in under the roof of the smithy. That brick box furnace got hotter than ever before that day, hot enough to burn a hole through the side. I believe the mist created a hydrogen/oxygen, super-charging effect. I had allowed borax to build up in the bottom of the box, the extra heat caused the borax to find a way out and it took part of the bricks with it.

One way to judge the welding temperature is with a metal coat hanger. Straighten it out but bend a little bit of the end at a right angle. Bring the billet up to where it looks wet, runny and dripty and stick the end of the

At the top a pattern-welded fixed blade exhibits a ladder pattern at the edge with a random pattern at the back. It has a snakewood handle and nickel silver guard. The folder at the bottom has a San Mai wire damascus blade, ironwood bolsters and a deer crown for a handle.

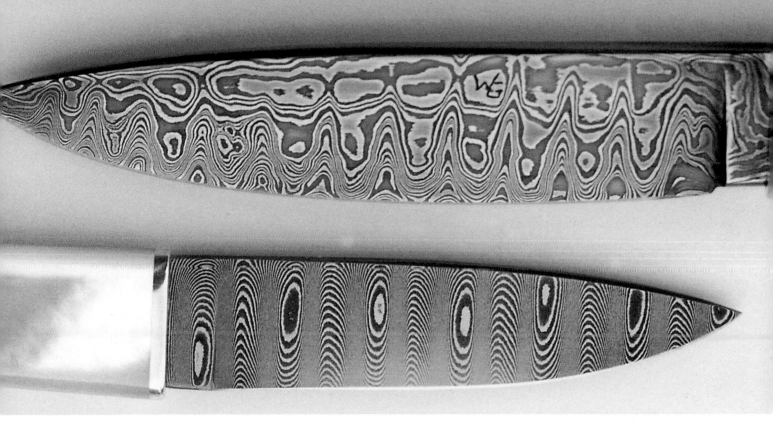

Two blades by the author. The top blade is random pattern welded at the back, incised at the edge. The bottom blade is stainless damascus made by Devin Thomas. It comes with the ladder pattern built in.

San Mai blade by the author. Wire damascus forms the outer skin, the core is bandsaw steel. Note how the hard core alternates with the wire damascus material at the edge.

hanger up against it. If the wire sticks to the billet you have a welding heat. Let the billet soak for two to four minutes, then take it out and hammer gently to get it started. If the coat hanger won't get unstuck, just forge it into the surface. It will usually be gone by time the billet is finished.

Pattern Development

I've not gotten into making a lot of the complicated patterns that can be developed. I adopted a style at the start and have pretty much stuck with that. I like the naturalness of the random pattern but have always thought that an incised pattern at the edge would improve the cutting ability. My style is to leave the random pattern in the back of the blade and develop a half-pattern at the edge.

San Mai

The most beautiful damascus blades do not always have good cutting ability. The solution for this is San Mai construction. San Mai means three layers and the way it works is to put the pretty stuff on the outside and a hard core in the center. San Mai welding is a good process to master because the resulting blades can have the best of everything. When I do a San Mai blade I usually do my version of a ladder pattern at the edge and that gives a tooth type pattern if all goes well. Keeping the core in the center of a San Mai blade is difficult and is one thing I am still trying to master.

Wire Damascus
Cable In History

Chinese and Egyptian workmen made rope of vines and rushes 5,000 years ago. Wire was first made 3,000 years ago, and the earliest known wire rope dates from about 700 BC. This rope was made of gold and silver and was used for ornamental purposes. In the ruins of Pompeii, a piece of bronze wire rope was found, 3/8-inch in diameter and 15 feet long: its use has never been determined. (Cable can also be made of vegetable fibers.) Steel cable is more properly called wire rope, so I will use its proper name from now on. Wire rope as we know it today was first made between 1816 and 1840; its production developed rapidly during the industrial expansion that followed the Civil War.

The History of Wire Rope Knives

Knives have been made out of forge-welded wire rope in Oregon for at least 115 years. I would imagine that once any scrap wire rope was available some enterprising

blacksmith forge-welded it to make knives and other tools. To my knowledge none of them developed patterns, etched it, or even realized that it had "damascus" properties. They only cared that it had the potential to make good knives. I have a collection of wire damascus knives and letter openers. Blacksmiths made the knives and only one of them is marked. The letter openers and one steel eraser are advertising items from wire rope companies. I have seen a cold chisel, hole punch and a screwdriver made out of the material. I have heard of a miner's pick, woodworking chisels and plane irons made out of it.

My Curiosity About Forge Welding

In 1954 I found a broad-ax on the desert in Idaho. I showed it to an old timer who was the local expert on old tools and knives. Ralph ran a second-hand store and I did a lot of knife trading with him. The ax was marked W. E. Beatty and Son, Warranted Cast Steel, Chester PA. Ralph couldn't help me with the exact age but he classed it as "old." He explained how the ax had been made by forge welding a steel bit in between the wrought iron body. The weld line was clearly visible and that made me all the more curious about the process of forge welding.

I still had that ax 10 years later when I met a retired railroad blacksmith named Tiny Alloway. I showed it to him and asked for more details on the process of forge welding. He was able to adequately explain the process and that's how he got on the subject of knives made out of cable, (wire rope). Tiny told me that there was a blacksmith in Albany-Salem area (that's just north of Eugene, Oregon) who was famous for his knives made of cable. I knew then that I wanted to make a knife out of wire but it was nearly 20 years before I got the chance.

I never learned anything else about the blacksmith who made knives out of cable, but one of the knives in my collection came out of that area. It is made of a single strand taken from a large wire rope. See the photo.

My First Wire Damascus

I worked with Bill Harsey at his shop in 1983 to make my first pattern-welded steel. He had a homemade gas forge and had made several pattern-welded damascus blades before we got acquainted. We wore ourselves out using a sledgehammer to get a pattern-welded billet up to 16 layers. It wasn't much, but it was a start.

Several years earlier Bill had made a blade out of

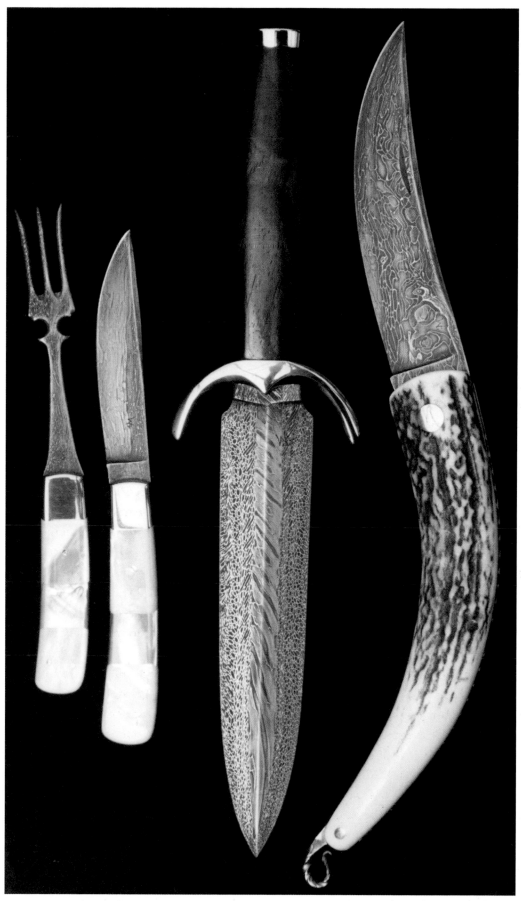

The finished dagger has three friends. The large folder has an elk brow tine for a handle, wire damascus blade.
The knife and fork have wire damascus blades, pearl handles and nickel silver bolsters.

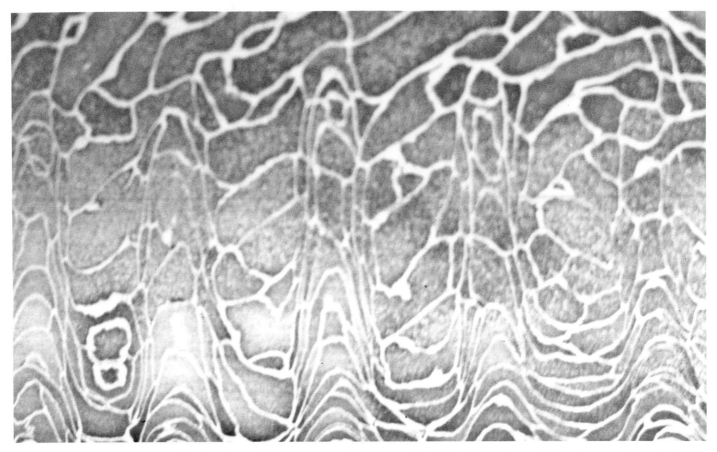

Close-up of a wire damascus blade where all the wires are the same alloy. Note the pattern at the edge made by first incising and then forging it flat.

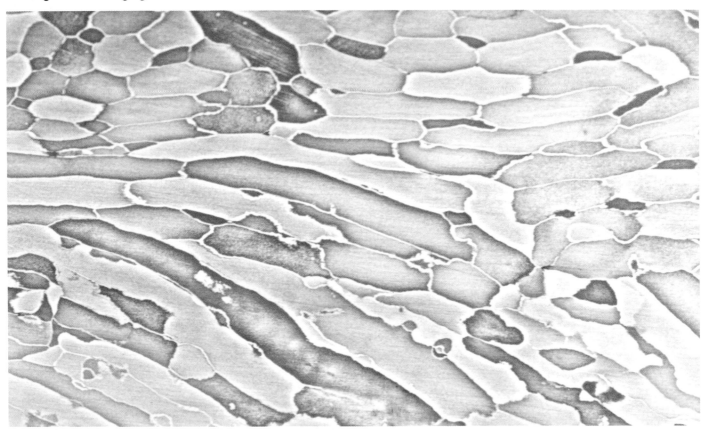

Close-up view of a wire damascus blade that is made from wire rope that has wires of three different alloy content.

wire rope. Like me, he had heard of the process from an old-timer. At that time I was getting my backyard smithy set up at home to work with coal. One of my first welded blades was made of wire rope. I named my new damascus material "wire welded." The name wire damascus hadn't been invented at that time. I found that it could be forge-welded quite well, at least on the surface. The first weld on wire rope can be made at a lower temperature than the subsequent welds. It usually welds at a lower temperature than pattern-welded steel and that is because all of the wires are usually high-carbon steel. With pattern-welded steel the high-carbon and low-carbon layers have different melting points. The low-carbon requires more heat to weld to the high-carbon material. The fact that more heat is required to weld pattern-welded steel makes it more difficult to keep from burning the carbon out of the high-carbon layers.

I wondered if my blade made of wire would show any pattern when etched. Once etched, my wire-welded blades did have a damascus pattern and this immediately brought to mind a very big question. What makes the pattern? If all the wires are high-carbon steel, why the pattern?

It was several years before Pat Wall, metallurgist at Pacific Machinery and Tool Steel in Portland, Oregon solved the puzzle for me. See the note he wrote back in 1986 after doing a photomicrograph of the cross section of a wire damascus sample piece. I learned that decarburization of the material in the weld zone is what causes the pattern. This same phenomenon creates the great strength that properly welded wire damascus exhibits. This settled the argument of whether a blade made of forge-welded wire rope is a type of damascus steel. If pattern-welded damascus steel is a composite steel made up of forge-welded layers of iron and steel, then forge-welded wire rope fits the definition.

Back then (1985-86) pattern-welded steel was usually made of iron and high-carbon steel. As the forge-welding and doubling progresses, the carbon in the high-carbon layers migrates into the iron, and if this is carried on long enough, the migration will be complete. The blade will show a damascus pattern but might have no gain in strength resulting from hard and soft layers. At that time I was using mild steel or wrought iron and O-1 in my

Note from metallurgist Pat Wall confirming the presence of iron in welded blades that started with all high-carbon wires.

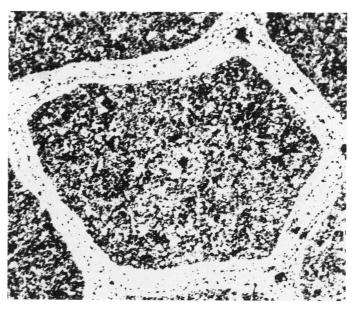

When I had photomicrographs made of the cross-section of welded-up high-carbon steel cable it showed a decarburized zone that was approximately .010-inches thick. This decarburized material is nearly pure iron. The carbon burned out during the welding heat; the higher the temperature and the more time at the welding heat, the more loss. The thickness of the shell of decarburized material around a small wire will be the same as in a large wire. The remaining percentage of high-carbon material is much greater as the diameter of the wire increases. (Magnified gazillions of times.)

The starting billet to weld up a composite bar dagger with a wire damascus blade. A single strand of the bridge cable at the left was removed. Every other wire was removed from the strand and replaced with an iron wire. The strand was twisted tight, welded, shaped into the bullet shape. The outer piece is 3/8-inch welded and doubled, forged in to a square bar and wrapped around the core.

pattern-welded blades. I was working them up to 500 layers but they did not show the flexibility that I expected of damascus steel. The blades were pretty but that's about all. On the other hand, my blades welded up from wire had great flexibility at a fairly high hardness.

Introducing Wire Damascus To The Knife World

I took my blades made of wire to most of the major knife shows in 1983. No one had seen it with the whole process explained with text and demonstration pieces.

I soon found that the pattern-welded world did not want to accept that steel made from wire could be "damascus steel." I wrote an article on how to do it in 1985. That article appeared in *Knives '86* which was released in November 1985. That article got dozens of folks making and experimenting with the material. I organized an informal "Wire Damascus Society." To be a member all someone had to do was make the material and believe in it. After kicking around several different names

I had the society vote on it and the decision was for wire damascus. I wrote a follow-up article in *Knives '87* and by then the material was well on its way to being accepted as a legitimate type of damascus material.

My fight to establish wire blades as a true type of damascus steel came from my test comparisons with pattern-welded steel. The wire blades had every property of pattern-welded steel, plus many advantages in strength. I wasn't interested in anyone's rules; the material itself was worth the effort to share it with the world.

Wire Damascus; A Misunderstood Material

Wire damascus is a misunderstood material by many makers. I've heard it said that it is "easy" damascus material. While it may seem easy to weld, the hard part is getting blades that are free of flaws. It's also very easy to end up with a blade that doesn't get hard enough to hold an edge. It will make the ultimate blade when it comes to flexible strength but it isn't easy to get there and still have

The author's collection of old wire damascus knives. The third knife from the top is the only one that is marked. It says "A. Cochran, 114 WIRES WELDED". The stamping is interesting because the words WIRES and WELDED are stamped with a single stamp. Whoever made this knife went to the extra expense to have stamps made to mark his work. The second knife from the bottom is the one that supposedly came out of the Albany area; "... there was a blacksmith famous for his knives made of cable", quote from Tiny Alloway, 1964. I got started on this collection with the second knife from the top. The end was cut with a hot chisel, it's not broken. Well-known tool collector Jack Birky found it in a box of old tools.

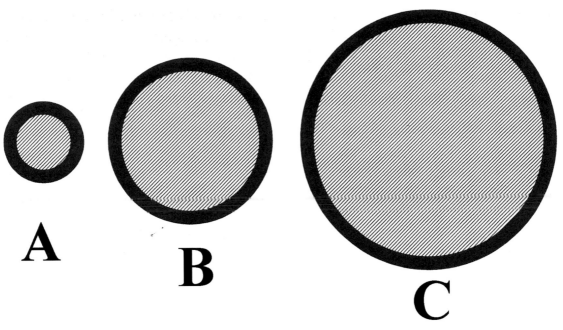

Each circle illustrates the cross section of a single wire from a welded-up blade made of high-carbon wire rope. The dark band is decarburized material. "A" is a small wire from 1/4-inch cable. When welded, it has more iron than steel in it. "B" is a medium-size wire from 1-inch cable. It has a lot more steel than iron, which makes a good balance of carbon content and pattern. "C" is an extra-large wire from a bridge cable. It has the maximum amount of steel remaining but blades made from this cable will not show much pattern or other characteristics that are expected in a damascus blade.

enough hardness to stay sharp with the best. The problem is the same with all types of forge-welded damascus; we work it in order to end up with beauty, flexible strength and cutting ability at the same time.

Automatic Layers

Steel, at the welding temperature, decarburizes at a rate of about .062 inch per hour. The carbon in a composite blade also moves, (diffuses is the metallurgical term). At the welding temperature it moves at the same rate of .062-inch per hour. The carbon always goes from the areas of high concentration to areas of low carbon. The rate of decarburization in forge welding must be the same. Measurements taken in sample pieces show the decarburized material to be approximately .005-inch deep. If the formula of .062-inch per hour is rounded off to .001-inch per minute, it works out to the actual amount of time that the work was at the welding temperature. Damascus blades can be folded so many times that there is no real difference in the carbon content between the layers. The blade may have a beautiful pattern but it is only because of the alloy content. I've made wire damascus blades that had so many wires that when forged down the appearance was like that of pattern-welded steel.

As high-carbon wires are forge-welded together the decarburization process causes a matrix of nearly pure iron to form in the area of coalescence (weld zone). This soft matrix weaves in, out, around and about, crossing and crisscrossing throughout the blade. This creates the typical pattern of a series of cells or scales. Unlike the flaws found in layered steel that can run a great distance, the flaws found in wire damascus are usually small and do not go too far. The exception would be a large flaw from a doubling weld. The very nature of wire damascus indicates the potential to make a more flexible blade than one with straight layers.

Different Wire, Different Results

Consider the possibilities with wires of different diameters. Quarter-inch diameter wire rope is usually made up of individual wires that are .015 inches in diameter. If the outer part of the wire is decarburized to a depth of .005 inches, it leaves a core of high-carbon material that is .005 inches thick. Figuring the surface area, there would be eight times more decarburized material than high-carbon material. Spectrographic testing of a welded-up blade made of 1/4-inch wires showed an overall remaining carbon content of 0.30, or a loss of nearly 60 percent of the carbon. While this is not as much as the theoretical loss figured above, it is enough loss that the blade would have poor edge-holding ability, but having exceptional strength.

Spectrographic testing of blades made from wire

rope with larger wires showed a much lower percentage loss of carbon. I will assume that the wire rope used in the following tests was 0.85 carbon. The blade made from 9/16-inch rope had a remaining carbon content of 0.65, while the one made from 1/2-inch rope had a remaining carbon content of 0.43.

Most wire rope is made of cold-drawn plow steel, which is simple high-carbon steel with .70 percent manganese. The carbon and alloy content are modified to give the desired strength. The cold drawing of the wires improves the physical characteristics, improves the tensile strength and transforms the natural grain of the steel to a fibrous structure. The fibrous nature of the wires is part of what imparts exceptional strength to wire rope.

Grades Of Wire Rope

There are eight basic grades of wire rope, see the table. Note the X, XX and XXX grades. These three grades have no more carbon, but gain their strength from the addition of chromium, vanadium or columbium.

Some of my favorite wire rope is 10 by 19 rotation-resistant rope that has all high-carbon wires, but with three different alloys. When etched these blades show three different color cells, indicating a difference of alloy content between the different wires. The wires are medium-sized so the edge-holding ability isn't good enough for a hunting knife but just about right for a dagger, boot knife or a tactical knife.

Quench Test All Wire Rope

Wire rope should be quench-tested to determine the makeup of the wires. The material to be tested should be heated to a point where it loses the ability to attract a magnet. Let the temperature climb just a little more and quench in oil or water. The sample should come out as hard as glass; anything else would be of dubious value to make a good knife. The majority of wire ropes will have wires of all the same material. There are exceptions and the quench test is just too simple to be passed up. Occasionally the outer strands will have wires of three different carbon contents. I have found extra-improved ropes to have low-carbon cores. When either a low-carbon or iron core is found, the outer strands can be unwound just enough to get the core out and then the wire rope is rewound.

Preparing Wire Rope For Welding

When working without a press or power hammer start out with 5/8-inch or 3/4-inch wire rope. It will be easier to work than the larger sizes. Save the larger wire rope for later when your skill is better. Work with pre-cut lengths no longer than 12 to 18 inches and arc- or gas-weld the ends up solid before starting. This keeps the wires from unwinding during the twisting and forge welding. The orange-hot rope should be twisted up as tight as possible. This causes the strands to cross more often, tightens up the pattern, and in general makes a better blade.

GRADE	CARBON	MANGANESE	TENSILE STRENGTH
IRON	.05-.15	?	82,00
PSI TRACTION STEEL	.20-.50	/	99,000
MILD PLOW STEEL	.40-70	?	143,000
PLOW STEEL	.60-.80	.70	180,000
IMPROVED PLOW STEEL	.70-.85	.70	195,000
EXTRA IMPROVED PLOW STEEL	*.85	.70	225,000
EXTRA, EXTRA IMPROVED PLOW STEEL	*.85	.70	?
EXTRA,EXTRA,EXTRA IMPROVED PLOW STEEL	*.85	.70	?

Wire Rope Grades

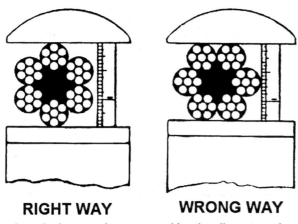

RIGHT WAY   **WRONG WAY**

The size of wire rope is measured by the diameter of a circle that will encompass it.

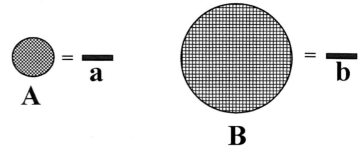

"A" represents a single piece of wire rope, "B" represents a bundle of wire rope pieces. When both are forge-welded and drawn into the same size billet the larger of the two will be more completely welded and make a much better blade.

My favorite starting stack is four pieces of 1-inch with a piece of 3/8-inch down the middle. The top view is of the wire end. The bottom is partially welded piece that I cut off of a billet I was making for a sword. I started with more than I needed because I didn't know the exact length necessary for a 20-inch blade.

Wire rope is treated with some type of tar-based heavy grease, which protects it from rust and lubricates it. This has to be removed before putting it in a welding fire. The best way to get it out is to burn it out but please check with your local air pollution authority to see if this is legal in your area. When I burned coal I would build a fire with dirty coke and use the already contaminated fire to burn the lubrication out. Now that I am welding with gas, I use the gas forge to burn out the lubrication. Start by putting in several pieces of wire rope at a time as the forge heats up to around 1,400 degrees F. As the steel heats up, the lubrication will start to burn off and there will be a lot of smoke coming out of the forge. The lubrication burning off is actually helping to fuel the fire and the smoke is caused by unburned fuel. At this time the gas can be turned back, but not off, and most of the smoke will be eliminated. If

you put too much wire in the forge at one time you will have massive amounts of smoke, and no cure for it.

Welding The Billet

Heat slowly and as uniformly as possible, wire-brush and flux with anhydrous borax before a scaling heat is reached. If you are not using anhydrous borax and getting good results, you are a good smith. If you are having problems with bad welds, a switch to anhydrous borax will probably solve the problem.

When you think you have a welding heat, using a light hammer and with rapid blows, and working as quickly as possible, work the hot mushy wires into a square bar. Work the billet on all sides, switching to a heavier hammer as it starts to solidify. It takes a lot of heavy hammering to get all the wires welded to each other. It usually takes me three or four heats to get a piece welded up solid, the final welding heat is used to work the billet into a rectangle. The gap where the wires meet on the outer surface is hard to get closed up. Even when worked under a heavy power hammer, the wrinkles just keep getting pushed down into the billet. I always rough grind the flats before the final welding heat. This gives you a chance to inspect the quality of the forge welding. After the final heat it is also edge ground and inspected for bad welds. If it appears to be not completely welded up, I will do another welding heat, working it into its finished shape.

Once you have mastered the welding of a single piece of cable you will want to move on to making larger pieces and composite blades. The majority of the wire damascus blades that I make today are made of multiple pieces stacked together and then forge-welded. I use either the whole pieces of rope or selected strands taken out of a rope. I have done many composite blades and I often use wire damascus for the outside and insert a tool steel core to make the cutting edge. At other times I will wrap a piece of low-carbon wire damascus around a core that was welded up of higher carbon wire. The soft core runs through the blade from front to back. This makes a very beautiful blade and it will have superior flexible strength at the same time. See the photo.

I use a hydraulic press for welding and although it's not as fast as a power hammer I like the control I have when working a wire or chain billet corner to corner. My backyard smithy is in a residential neighborhood and so I could not run a power hammer. The press makes less noise than a lawnmower and I've never had a complaint from a neighbor. The first welds are made between flat dies. Subsequent welds are made with drawing dies and then the flat ones are used for getting the billet straightened up. I need to make a closed "swage" type spring die setup because it would speed up the welding on some types of wire and chain billets.

My starting billet is usually 3 or 4 inches long and 2 inches wide and 4 inches high. The 2-inch by 4-inch billet will make as many as four fixed-blade knives. I like working big billets because I can make more material in less time. My first welding heat works the 2 by 4 billet into a square. With the next welding heat, the reduction with the press is corner to corner. The next heat will be used to reduce the thickness and then back to a corner-to-corner weld. I want to push the wires together from every possible angle. When a wire billet is worked on the square or rectangle only, the corners may not get enough pressure to be perfectly welded. When the starting billet stretches out to about 12 inches I usually cut it in half to finish taking it down to blade shapes.

A properly welded blade made from wire rope should appear as a solid piece of steel with very few flaws. (That's prior to etching.) I've been specializing in "wire Damascus" for a long time and in my opinion when there are flaws in a wire blade it is caused because some of the wires did not get pushed up against all the other wires while it was at the welding heat. (That opinion is based on the assumption that the billet was subjected to proper welding heats.)

Tamping

Wire rope has wires running in all directions and every angle that can be imagined. Perhaps some unexplained flaws are caused because the wires didn't get pushed together at the exact angle necessary for contact. A tamping action at the welding heat might help eliminate some small flaws that are otherwise hard to explain. I got the idea for a tamping weld while watching a video of some European smiths working. They were welding up lots of squares and rectangles of scrap to make a plowshare. They started with a box-like container on a handle and carefully filled it with the scrap pieces. The container was brought up to the welding heat and the sides of the billet were hit with a drop hammer. It was also tamped on its end at the welding heat and I assumed it was to insure that butted-up ends welded together. If the ends didn't make contact at the welding heat they might not have stuck together. It's something to think about and I will try it soon.

No-Fold Wire Damascus

I don't fold my normal billets of wire rope. When a billet is folded there is the chance for a flaw, sometimes a big one. A more important reason is that wire takes a tremendous reduction in cross section to completely weld up. That's why I start with a big bundle and work all the way to the blade shape by taking welding heats on it each time. I came to this method by cross-sectioning billets and examining them with a microscope to see if they were completely welded. The greater the reduction in size at the welding heat, the less flaws will be found in the blade. It appears that the outside of the billet welds up before the center. As reduction occurs the center portion becomes more solid.

Forging Damascus

If the ends were arc or gas-welded prior to twisting, be sure to cut or grind off that part before forging the point on the blade. The rule here is to keep it hot and forge very close to shape. I work my wire blades down very close to the finished shape with welding heats. The reason for forging close to shape is the outside of a billet is more apt to be completely welded. As the billet is ground there is more chance of getting into an area that contains flaws. When the blade is completely forged to shape it should be normalized and annealed before rough grinding and heat-treating.

Heat Treating For Wire Damascus

Consider that each wire damascus blade is an individual and should be treated as such. Almost any type of oil will work to harden wire damascus. Any quench oil for knife work should be heated to around 130 to 140 degrees F. Temper immediately at 300 to 450 degrees F depending on the as-quenched hardness and intended use.

The two tough guys are my grandsons Justin and Jeff in 1991. It was Halloween time, I had just finished the sword and sheath and I thought they would look good with it in their ninja costumes. Justin is holding the sword, Jeff the sheath. They're all grown up now, time sure flies by when you're having fun.

Blades made of fine wires will not be as hard as those made from larger wires, and will not require much more than a stress relief draw of 300 degrees F. Temper all blades three times for at least 90 minutes.

See the chapter on heat-treating.

Etching Damascus Steel

For proper etching, the blade will have to be flat and free of scratches. If there are any rough grinding marks or ripples left in the blade they will show up in the finished blade. I use a 400- to 600-grit hand-rubbed finish to go into the first etch. I don't like the appearance of a buffed damascus blade because it washes out pattern. I use hand rubbing all the way through; the final finish is done with 1,500-grit or finer paper.

The strength of the etchant is very important. If it is too strong it will cut the whole blade down and the pattern will not have as much definition as it could have. I used an acid etch for my first blades and the results were not too bad. I tried ferric chloride and it worked so well that I have not tried anything else. Radio Shack stores sell ferric chloride in a 16-ounce bottle that says "ARCHER ETCHANT." The contents of the bottle should be mixed with three to four parts of water. In warm weather I get a good etch without heating the etch solution. In the wintertime when the shop temperature is around 55 to 60 degrees F I heat the etch bath to 70 to 80 degrees F. When heated it gives a slightly different etch, you will want to experiment to get results you are happy with.

A slow etch will almost always give a better pattern. When the etch looks ragged and pitted, the etchant is too strong and needs more water. I get the best results by etching several times, and hand rubbing with 1,200-grit paper in between etches.

Some blades will not have as much contrast as others do. These can be treated with a cold blue solution after etching. They are then rubbed out with your finest grit paper. The best cold blue product I've found is Birchwood Casey Super Blue. Don't settle for anything else. The object of the cold blue treatment followed by light rubbing is to color the deep part of the pattern and leave the high part shiny. Follow the directions on the container and after the process is done take the finest paper you have, 1,500-grit will do, and give the high parts a rub to shine them up. A stiff, but not too hard, backing is good behind the paper. If a finger is used the polishing paper may get pushed down in the deep part of the pattern and the results won't be sharp and crisp.

When I am satisfied with the finish I put the blade under a light bulb used to warm epoxy to 90 degrees F. When the blade is warm it is rubbed down with either WD-40 or Liquid Wrench. I will let the blade sit for a while and then wipe it dry. The oil treatment helps set the color and seal the surface.

This stag-crown folder is an example of the beautiful knives that can be made with tools from a $50 knife shop.

CHAPTER 7

HOMEMADE GRINDERS

The Good News Grinder

See the photo. It's not much of a grinder when compared to the store-bought type. The good news is that it will make finishing a blade about 1,000 percent faster and easier than doing it all by hand. I built the grinder for about $5 and about an hour and a half of labor. (Most of that time was spent wiring in a switch and a grounded electrical cord.) It's an exact replica of the first grinder I built back in 1963. Although it wasn't much of a machine, it worked well enough to grind out my first knife and there were those who liked that knife well enough to have me make one like it for them. I made the first dozen or so knives with that original grinder. I then built one that used a double-ended pillow block arbor and a 1-hp motor. That Good News Grinder then became a full-time buffing machine.

The Good News Grinder.

This is the project knife for the Krause Publications' book, BLADE's® Guide To Making Knives. I used the Good News Grinder exclusively in the making of this knife.

Homemade belt grinder of the upright type, it's going strong after 21 years of constant use. Original cost of all parts was less than $75.

Details of the homemade 2 by 72 grinder.

blades with it and the wheel did not need dressing. That is truly an amazing wheel compared to the poor quality store-bought wheel I used back in 1963. The SG wheel started at 12 inches and when worn down to 9 inches on a saw gumming machine it was no longer efficient and was discarded. I got it in a trade with another maker.

I didn't retire the Good News Grinder after I finished *The $50 Knife Shop* magazine series for *BLADE®* and the first edition of this book. I set it up with an abrasive cut-off wheel and it got a lot of use at a workshop I taught in Washington State. I recently used the good news grinder to make the project knife for the Krause Publications' book *BLADE®'s Guide To Making Knives*. The holder for the work rest has been modified to make it stronger and I've added a garage sale chuck and sanding disc to make it more versatile.

Introduction To Belt Grinders

One hundred years ago the only things needed to shape a knife were a forge, anvil, hammer and some tongs. A worn-out file would do just fine for blade material. Refining the shape of the blade prior to quenching was done with a file and perhaps a foot-powered grindstone. The blade was heated for quenching in the forge fire and then quenched in water or animal fat of some type. Tempering was done with the heat from the forge. The grindstone probably created the final finish on the blade. Any old deer antler would work for a handle to finish off the knife.

Since that time, man has walked on the moon and sent a miniature dune buggy to Mars. Today's civilization is in an age of "hi-tech" and most knifemakers would not think of trying to produce their product without a belt grinder. I made 300 knives in the 1960s without a belt grinder. I wasn't trying to prove anything; I just didn't know any better. When I got started there were no knife magazines to tell me how to do it. There were no knifemakers around for me to learn from until I got some started. I just went ahead and did it with what I had, and that wasn't much.

The average knife shop in the 1970s had one relatively simple belt grinder. The modern knifemaker's shop might have two or more belt grinders, and at least one will be the latest model with a variable-speed motor. I have three homemade grinders and two that were commercially made; each one was designed or purchased for a specific purpose. I suppose I could get by with two but it is more

More good news is that this grinder was made of 100 percent recycled stuff from thrift stores and yard sales. Parts are as follows: 1950s-style Westinghouse 1/3-hp, 1,750-rpm washing machine motor; a grinding wheel adapter like the one from Sears with a worn out saw-sharpening wheel on it. The base is scrap plywood, and an old cookie sheet was used for a guard.

The reconstruction of my first grinder works amazingly well considering it is somewhat under-powered and runs at half the speed of most "real" bench grinders. The secret is the Norton SG wheel, which removes steel very efficiently. Norton describes the SG abrasive as having a sub-micron crystal structure with billions of particles in each grain. During grinding the grain resharpens itself, continually exposing fresh, sharp cutting points. It works, I ground two efficient to have a different one set up for each of the many types of grinding that are required to complete a knife.

So what is so complicated about a belt grinder? It starts with a motor that has either a drive wheel or pulley that fits onto the shaft. If the motor has a wheel, it drives the abrasive belt. If the motor has a pulley, it drives a V belt that goes to a pulley that either drives a contact wheel or drive wheel. There is almost always another wheel that keeps the belt going in a straight line; it's called a tracking wheel. Finally, there is either a platen or a third contact wheel for the belt to run against so that the object to be shaped can be applied to the speeding grit.

A belt grinder fabricated from standard steel shapes is a very simple piece of equipment. (See photo) Note that the frame and platen supports are all standard sizes of flat bar, angle and C channel steel. The placement of the top platen support bracket is essential for the mounting of many of my specialty jigs. All of the other "stuff" in-between is only there to hold the three or four important parts together and provide a means of mounting attachments, guards or whatever. It is difficult to make custom set-ups on most commercial machines because of the complicated cast shapes they are made of.

The Disadvantages Of Making Your Own Grinder

Building a belt grinder is not for everyone. When the life span of a first-class commercial grinder is considered, 20+ years, the initial cost is a bargain. The homemade grinder can become very expensive when the time involved is considered. The design has to be worked out and all the parts chased down. Once all of the materials are on hand the parts have to be shaped, drilled and then bolted together. Welding can cause warping and twisting of the frame and that is not good. The ability to make adjustments is essential, especially at the points where the platen attaches. All that in-between stuff must hold the contact wheel and platen in near perfect alignment with each other and the drive wheel. Bolted-together construction is best because shims can be used to keep everything in alignment. The advantage of building your own grinder from scratch is that it can be made more versatile and tailor-made to the types of grinds being done.

Two Basic Groups of Grinders

Belt grinders suitable for knife work can be divided into two basic groups: two-wheel and three-wheel. The type of blades being made will determine the best type of grinder. Flat, convex and slack belt work is best done on a two-wheel machine. The platen on a two-wheel machine is usually twice as long as that provided with the platen attachment for a three-wheel machine and longer is usually better, especially when grinding long blades.

A two-wheel machine can be either horizontal or vertical. (See figures 1 and 2.) This type usually has a platen and square table attachment, some have a disk. They may or may not be constructed so that the drive wheel is also a contact wheel for grinding.

The easiest to build and most useful grinder is a vertical two-wheel machine. I rarely do hollow-ground knives so I do 99 percent of my blade work on a two-wheel, vertical platen machine.

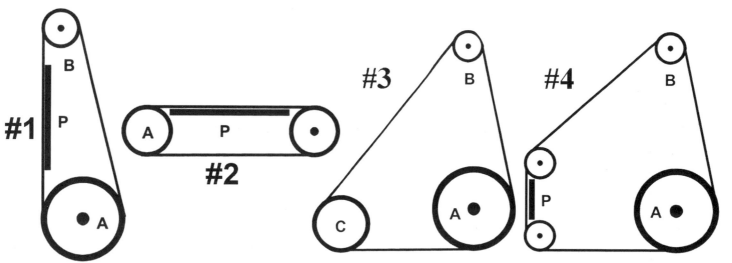

#1 a vertical platen grinder and #2 a horizontal two-wheel grinder.

#3 shows the layout of a three-wheel grinder with a contact wheel out in front. #4 shows the same basic machine set up with a platen attachment.

A three-wheel machine is the best choice for hollow grinding and by changing wheels a number of different grinds can be made. When the platen attachment is installed on a three-wheel machine, it will then have four wheels. (See figures 3 and 4.)

Anatomy of A Belt Grinder

With a three-wheel grinder the power is transferred from the motor to the abrasive belt by the drive wheel. (See part A in 3 and 4.) The idler wheel is usually where the tracking device is and usually furnishes the tension on the belt. (See part B.) The contact wheel is designed to "contact" the work; its main duties are rough shaping and hollow grinding. It may be serrated or smooth and will vary in hardness depending on the type of grinding. (See part C.)

The work is made flat by being held against the belt as it passes over the platen. (See part P.) A platen machine usually has a worktable that either swings into position or is bolted on for square grinding (90-degrees from the platen), such as in profiling blades. Shaped platens are useful for specialty grinding. I have one that duplicates the hollow grind made with a 20-inch contact wheel. A different one creates an exact convex shape to the blade. See the illustrations.

Commercial Grinders

Most commercial grinders are made of complicated castings because that is the economical way to mass-produce machines. I chose the Wilton Square Wheel Grinder to dissect because it has been around as long or longer than most of the other machines used by knifemakers. It is a production-quality machine and quite versatile. The Square Wheel grinder also has a lot of cast parts and that makes it perfect for my examination. It is not uncommon for a relatively simple cast part to cost over $100.

I made a list of the 28 major parts of the Square Wheel Grinder and the total was close to $1,700. Subtracting all the in-between parts that can be made of standard steel shapes lowered the price to about $500. The bottom line is that a first-class grinder can be made for one-third the cost of a manufactured one.

I like to break things down to small units. So, what would a new commercial grinder cost per day over a 20-year period? I'll buy a really good one, $2,000 worth of good parts. That would be $200 per year, $16 per month and approximately 55-cents per day.

The $16 Grinder

There are those who believe that a 1-inch by 42-inch grinder is a waste of time and money. I'd say that was true if a new one were being considered. Most commercial narrow belt sanders are not much as a grinder. The $100 or more could be spent on parts to build a 2-inch by 72-inch model. So, if the best grinder for making blades is a 2 by 72, why build a 1 by 42 grinder?

Advantages of the 1 by 42 grinder:

1) A smaller motor will work just fine for this size belt. The 1/2-hp motors are more readily available and less expensive than the larger motor required for 2-inch-wide belts. A 1/2-hp motor driving a 1-inch belt has the same grinding power as a 1-hp motor on a 2-inch wide-belt.
2) The smaller physical size makes fabrication easier.
3) In several ways the 1-inch-wide belt is better for short blades.
4) Makeshift wheels that are 1-inch wide are easier to find than the 2-inch variety.
5) I've found that a properly designed 1 by 42 will do a variety of jobs very well.

Disadvantages of the 1 by 42

1) Butt-spliced, high-quality belts are somewhat harder to find. (Butt splices don't go "bump" under the blade as they go.)
2) The small belts may not be as efficient in belt cost
3) The majority of commercial 1 by 42 grinders are not suitable for knife work. The platen and square table set-ups are poorly designed and there is no provision for grinding with a contact wheel.

Grinder Motors

The place to start when designing a grinder is with the motor. I dug around in my junk piles and found a motor from a 1950s gasoline pump. Such a motor is explosion proof, which means sparks and dust cannot get into it. This makes them very dependable for grinders and buffing machines. I bought that motor for $5 at a yard sale 25 years ago and have used it mostly to power a buffing wheel since then. This type of motor does not need a cooling fan because it is heavily built with a lot of copper in it. That translates as having the ability to absorb overloading.

Most modern, open-frame motors will not last long on

The $16 Grinder

a grinder. Wood and metal dust get into the windings in the motor and, when enough dust accumulates and a spark ignites it, the motor will burn up before it can be shut down. A sealed motor with an external cooling fan (TEFC) is the most suitable for use on a grinder. Old and heavy motors that do not have a starting capacitor will often start a belt grinder just fine. The modern, lightweight motors usually need to be of the capacitor-start type.

Design It As You Build It

The motor should be securely bolted to a heavy base. This design has a V-belt drive to the arbor. With the pulley in place on the motor, hold the drive belt in the position that it will run and make some rough measurements for location of the arbor. With the arbor mounted to the base and the drive wheel in place, mark the location for the center support. The height of the center support is

The $16 grinder set up with a disk.

determined by holding a belt onto the drive wheel and measuring to the approximate location of the tracking/idler wheel. Drill the holes for the top arm and platen supports, then mount the center support and install it. The top arm is cut roughly to shape and the idler/tracking wheel installed. With the spring holding tension on the belt, the platen support brackets can be cut to shape and the platen fabricated and installed. The bracket that holds the square table is riveted to the platen so that arc welding, or drilling and tapping was eliminated. I haven't given any dimensions because your stuff is not going to be the same as what I used. The idea is to use what you have available.

The base for the machine and all the major parts are Oregon maple, remnants from a cabinet shop. The tools used to build the $16 grinder were a band saw, drill press and electric drill. Some woodwork was done with another homemade belt grinder but all of it could have been done by hand. I spent about eight hours building it. It's a very nice little machine for knife work and actually quite powerful for rough grinding with coarse belts.

Belt Speed

The revolutions per minute (rpm) of the motor will determine the drive-wheel speed to give the desired surface feet per minute (sfm). A three-wheel machine can use either a 1,750- or 3,600-rpm motor. The drive-wheel diameter is changed to give the desired belt speed. A two-wheel machine should be 1,750 rpm with an 8-inch drive/contact wheel. This gives clearance to grind on the drive wheel.

The $16 grinder has a one-to-one pulley ratio from the motor to the arbor. At 1,750 rpm, the 6-inch drive/contact wheel moves the belt along at approximately 2,700 sfm. An 8-inch drive wheel would be better but I didn't have one that slipped right onto the arbor. Most belt manufacturers recommend 5,000 sfm for the maximum in material removal. I am not in that much of a hurry so I run my machines more slowly. The slower speed gives me better control with less heat generated in a hardened blade.

The three-step pulley on the arbor could be utilized to make it a variable-speed grinder. Three speeds could be available with a single pulley on the motor. Nine speeds are possible with three-groove pulleys on both ends. The motor mount would have to be constructed so that the motor could be moved sideways and adjusted for belt length.

There is a big advantage of building a belt grinder on one end of a double-ended arbor. The second end can

Drive Wheel Diameter	Approximate SFM at 1750 RPM	Approximate SFM at 3400 RPM
3"	1,500	2,650
4"	1,850	3,550
5"	2,300	4,500
6"	2,750	5,300
8"	3,700	DANGER
9"	4,150	DANGER
10"	4,600	DANGER

Surface Feet Per Minute table.

Idler wheel and bearing detail.

be set up with a disk as shown in the photo, or perhaps a buffing wheel.

Tracking is provided by adjusting the tension on a large wing nut that is on the end of the bolt that the idle/ wheel support-arm pivots on. The hole in the top arm should be a bit sloppy on the bolt so that the tension of the belt and spring will cause the arm to rotate away from parallel with the upright. When the wing nut is tightened, it pulls the arm back toward parallel with the upright. Some adjustment by using shims on the frame may be necessary to get the alignment correct for this to work.

A Successful Project

I used the $16 grinder for six months and become quite used to having it next to my upright 2 by 72 machine. I keep it set up with a 120 ceramic belt and in the course of the average day it saves me a dozen belt-changes on the 2 by 72. I like the 1-inch-wide belt

1 by 42 built by the author about 25 years ago for a person who was starting a knife sharpening business. An industrial cart wheel was turned and balanced for use as a drive/contact wheel.

for many of the detail operations that are necessary in knifemaking. Holding a 1/2-inch-wide part against a 1-inch-wide belt is much easier than with a 2-inch-wide belt.

The $16 grinder was simple and quick for me to build because of my large inventory of found objects. My hope is that any mystery surrounding the design of belt grinders has been overcome by my successful experiment.

Using Junkyard Parts

My opinion is that an abrasive belt is not intelligent enough to know if it is being driven by a $150 contact wheel or an industrial cart-wheel that was rescued from a scrap yard. The important thing is that the wheel runs true and has good balance. This is especially true for hollow grinding. A store-bought contact wheel is a near necessity (and a good investment) if the grinder is to be used for making hollow-ground knives. For use as a roughing grinder for profiling blades, a little run-out is not that detrimental.

The drive wheel for the $16 grinder is from a hand truck and set me back $1. I got lucky with it because it ran amazingly true on the arbor. Out-of-true wheels must be turned or ground true on a lathe, or in place on the shaft on which they will run. The double-ended arbor was purchased at a yard sale for $10. The left side has been fitted with a disc-sanding attachment. A grinding wheel with an appropriate guard or a buffing wheel could also be used in that position.

The bearing for the idler/tracking wheel came from a water pump for a 1974 Honda automobile. When I replaced the leaking water pump, I realized that the bearing was still good; only the seal was bad. I saved that bearing for 15 years until the right rubber part came along. It happened that the rubber shock absorber from the weight section of a junked muscle-building machine slipped right onto it. The rubber is attached to the water pump bearing with Duro® brand Super-Glue®.

I've had many requests for information on how to locate reasonably priced wheels for drive and contact wheels. Most of mine are from industrial carts and I find new ones occasionally at yard and tool sales. Others are found on the aluminum pile at my favorite scrap yard. If digging around in scrap yards is not to your liking, check for new ones with industrial supply companies.

Everywhere that I've gone lately I looked for cart wheels. The first ones I found were on the carts at the local Costco Warehouse. My wife and I recently traveled by air to Hawaii for a vacation. Everywhere I looked I found wheels suitable for use for drive or contact wheels. The ones on the rental push-carts for luggage in the airports are nearly perfect and come in two sizes. I found some at the Battleship Arizona Memorial at Pearl Harbor. They were on one end of the gangplank on the U.S. Navy boat that took us out to the site. I'm making the point that with so many suitable wheels in use, many are going to have to be replaced and they end up in the scrap yard.

The Basic Two-Wheel Belt Grinder

The simplest belt grinder has only two wheels and that's the type I do most of my blade work on. This design evolved over a period of 28 years of making my own belt grinders and it's made exactly the way it is because of the

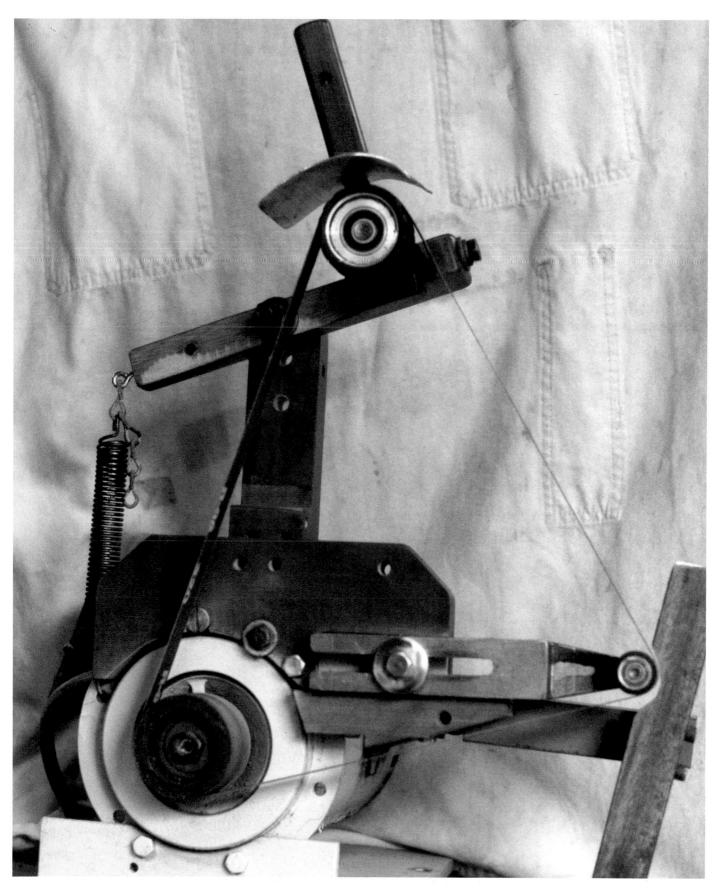

I use this 1 by 42 for many tasks. The 1-inch wheel stays out front for detail work 90 percent of the time. A pump motor from a commercial dishwasher powers it, the frame parts are 95 percent Micarta. Commercial wheels from Bader are at the top and out front. I have wheels up to 6 inches that will ride out front when needed. The drive wheel is from a skateboard that was fitted with a bronze bushing in the bore to fit the motor shaft, and then turned true on my lathe.

way I make knives. Most of the knives I make are either flat-or convex-ground and the upright machine is just right for that.

The three features that are used the most by a flat/convex blade grinder like me are the platen, square table and slack belt sections. The whole machine is built around those three features. My design has a nice long platen with slack-belt areas above and below. I'm constantly going from using the flat platen to the square table so it needs it to be quickly available. With a half turn of the bolt, the table is either in grinding position or swung out of the way. The worst grinder I ever used had three screws that had to be removed to go from the square table to flat grinding on the platen.

See the photo of my #1 using machine; built in 1984 and still running strong. Note the construction is all angle, channel and flat steel. The flat shapes and right angles make it easy to clamp or bolt on the many fixtures I have developed to make my knifemaking easier. Note the extension at the back to allow the machine to be mounted horizontally on a bench. My opinion is that belt grinders should be bolted rather than welded together. Welding has the habit of warping and twisting things out of alignment. Some shim adjustment is usually necessary to make a new machine track correctly. This is not possible when the frame is welded together.

The following is a description of the parts and features of this simple machine. 1) The motor is a totally enclosed, fancooled (TEFC) 1,750-rpm unit that gives 3,665 sfm with the 8-inch drive wheel. 2) The drive wheel is an 8-inch diameter lapidary wheel that I found at a flea market. It was 2-1/2 inches wide with cork glued onto the diameter. It had a ratchet-type mechanism that tightened a strip of abrasive cloth around the work surface. I stripped out the tightening mechanism, put it on a lathe and narrowed it up to 2 inches. Then I cleaned the cork off and used Barge Cement to glue neoprene onto the aluminum wheel. The folks at Goodyear who sold me the neoprene said that Barge cement wouldn't hold the rubber on the wheel and insisted that I buy their glue. I went ahead and used Barge because I had it on hand for gluing up my sheaths. The wheel has been running 21 years now with only one change of the neoprene. It didn't come loose; it just wore out. 3) The idler/tracking wheel is a section of the roller from a Maytag wringer washer. The white, natural rubber lasts for years and they are easy to machine. The

wringers have a steel center; I bored it out for a snug fit onto the end of the water pump bearing. A set screw holds the wheel in place. Note the sheet metal guard above the idler wheel, it helps to keeps grit and sparks out of my face. It's mounted on a hinge so it can be swung out of the way for changing belts.

For flattening blades the platen should be as long as is practical, mine is 12 inches and that gives clearance at both top and bottom for slack belt grinding. Should platen material be hard or soft? If you want it hard I'll not argue the point. I prefer mine to be made of mild steel because then I can draw file it occasionally to get it flat. If the platen is made of hard material it has to be ground flat each time it gets worn.

Make two identical platens for your new homemade grinder. They will need to be ground or milled flat when new. When the one on the machine becomes too worn to do good work, take it off, put the new one on and then grind the worn one flat. Put the newly ground one on the shelf and it will be ready to replace the one in use when it becomes worn. If you have a milling machine or surface grinder, or access to one, two platens are not necessary. I use a 6-inch by 48-inch Craftsman to grind my platens flat. The platen should mount from the center, not one side. This allows work to wrap around the platen to a degree that isn't possible with a side-mount.

A nice big square table is best because it furnishes better support when profiling large blades; mine is 3-1/2 inches by 7 Inches wide. Some of my attachments need the large area of the square table to be held securely in place. It should be designed so that by loosening one screw it will swing clear of the platen.

Big Red:
The Multi-purpose Grinder

Big Red came out of my need for a multi-purpose machine to take to demonstrations where a grinder was not available. I named Big Red before I found out the Dayton bench grinder I started out with was called "Big Red." I chose a double-ended grinder for a power supply so that I would have the option of setting up the second end with a variety of operations. Possible applications would be as a hard-wheel grinder or abrasive cut-off machine. Another time it might be used as a disc or drum sander.

Big Red was designed to be easily adaptable to use more than one size belt. When finished, he will be capable

The sparks are being made by one of those abrasive belts that isn't smart enough to know that it's being run by a lot of junkyard steel, a motor from a second-hand store and drive wheel that came from a flea market.

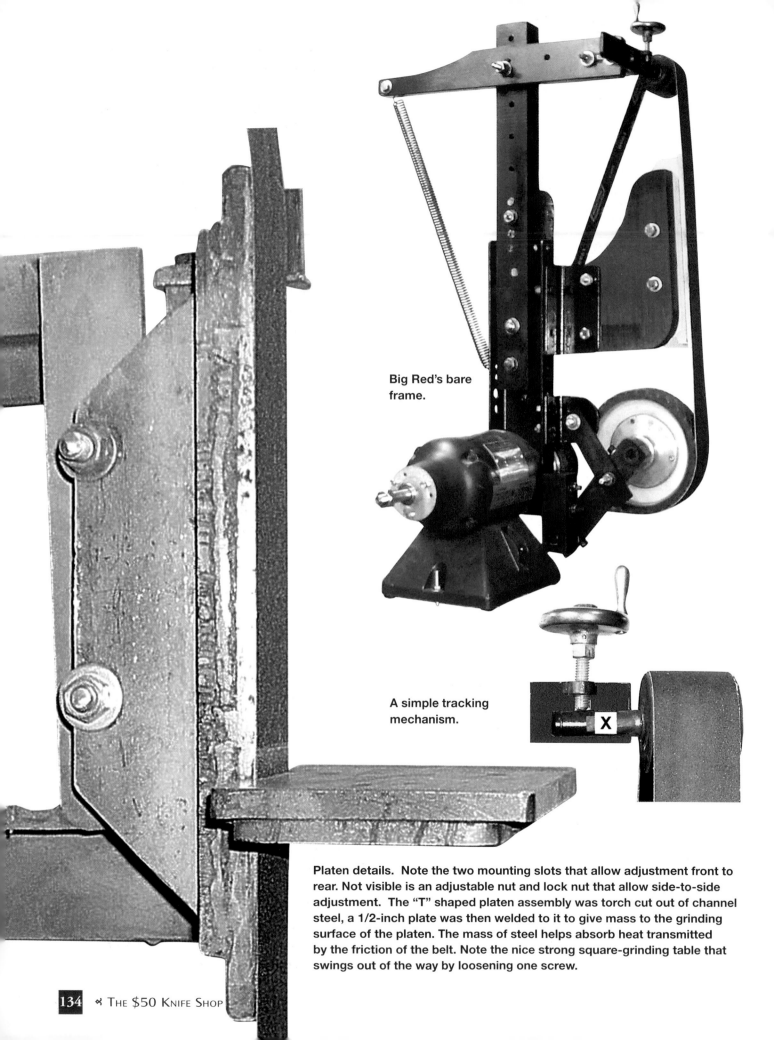

Big Red's bare frame.

A simple tracking mechanism.

Platen details. Note the two mounting slots that allow adjustment front to rear. Not visible is an adjustable nut and lock nut that allow side-to-side adjustment. The "T" shaped platen assembly was torch cut out of channel steel, a 1/2-inch plate was then welded to it to give mass to the grinding surface of the platen. The mass of steel helps absorb heat transmitted by the friction of the belt. Note the nice strong square-grinding table that swings out of the way by loosening one screw.

The adjusto arm.

The Dayton grinder known as "Big Red."

The Baldor® Grinder motor runs at 3,600 rpm. The 4.75-inch drive wheel came on a gear-motor that I bought at a yard sale for $10. I thought that was a pretty good deal, considering that it was a $250 unit when new. The drive wheel was out of round so I had to turn it on my antique lathe to get it running true and in balance. The 4.75-inch wheel will turn the belt at a rate of 4,710 sfm. That is a good speed for rough grinding but just a little fast for the way I like to work. My upright "Basic" machine runs at 3,665 sfm. It has a 1,750-rpm motor turning an 8-inch contact/drive wheel.

The tire for the serrated contact wheel was rescued from a scrap pile. It is of the type found on some Wilton Square Wheel Grinders. The hub came from another source and by pure luck they matched perfectly. This type wheel and hub will be found in most knifemakers' supply catalogs.

The tracking/contact wheel runs on a water-pump-type bearing. The diameter of the bearing housing is 1.181 inch, which is just undersize of 1-3/16 inches. The shaft is 5/16 inches in diameter. The bearing is the type found in many commercial contact wheels. The back of the bearing shaft is ground flat where it contacts the support bar. The X in the illustration shows the bolt head that makes the pivot point for the tracking adjustment. The rubber/steel rim was a remnant from a manufacturing operation. I bored it out for a press fit on the bearing. The rest of the picture explains itself.

Big Red Shows His Versatility

This picture shows the contact wheel setup for rough grinding with 2 by 48 belts. It is a quick and easy change to go from the 2 by 72 belt setup to the contact wheel with 2 by 48 belts. The adjusto-arm is moved down and the tracker/idler arm is lowered to the position shown. The tension spring is then hooked up to the top of the main support. I planned for this setup by drilling the necessary holes when I made the main support. I do not normally use 2 by 48 belts but I recently acquired a nice supply of 50-grit roughing belts at a dirt-cheap price. The "wheel-out-front" setup for 2 by 72 is made easily by moving the position of the tracker/idler arm up a notch or two on the main support.

of handling three belt sizes. The normal set-up will be for 2 by 72. A set-up of 1 by 42 will be used with small-diameter wheels for detail work. A set-up for 2 by 48 will be available to utilize a large number of roughing belts that I bought at a very low price.

By lowering the position of the top idler and swinging out the adjusto-bar, any size contact wheel can be mounted out front. (Note the extra holes in the upright support to allow lowering of the tracking wheel.) The adjusto-bar and its mounting bracket are made of Micarta. The range of adjustment will allow any diameter of wheel to run out front. Holders for the other types of contact wheels are easily fabricated. The channel-steel frame is bolted to the holes where the grinder guard was mounted. The extension and tracker-arm are made of maple. Note the extra holes in the frame to allow the adapters for the different-sized belts and the platen/square table assembly.

The Platen

The shot of Big Red at the start of the chapter shows the platen in place. The platen is the spare for my basic machine. Why change a perfect design? See my comments on platens in the previous section.

I make my platens in a T shape and of heavy stock. The leg of the T furnishes the mounting surface. This allows the maximum clearance on both sides of the platen. When a platen has lots of steel in it there is not as much distortion from heat, and it will outlive many flat grinding or machining jobs. The mounting bracket has two pieces of all-thread or long bolts with jam nuts in place. This allows the platen to be adjusted true with the line on which the belt runs.

Parts List For Big Red:

1. Main support, 4" X 21", "C" channel steel.
2. Tension spring. (It may have come from a dishwasher door.)
3. Main support extendo, maple 2" X 2-1/2" X 23".
4. Idler/tracker arm, maple 1" X 2-1/2" X 17".
5. Tracker mechanism.
6. Idler/tracker wheel.
7. Platen mounting bracket, maple 1-1/4" X 7" X 11".
8. Platen mounting bolt, 3/8" x whatever.
9. Platen, steel, 2" X 12".
10. Angle bracket, steel 3" X 6".
11. 2 by 72 Norton SG 60-grit abrasive belt. (The best!)
12. Adjusto brace bracket, steel angle, 3" X 3".
13. Adjusto brace, steel 1/4" X 1-1/2" X 7".
14. Adjusto bracket, Micarta, 1" X 2" X 5".
15. Mounting block, Micarta, 2" X 2" X 5"

Except for the Baldor grinder motor and contact wheels, Big Red grew out of my junk piles. Many of the parts are the size they are because that's the way I found them, that's just the way I do it. There is no reason to make the main support out of two different sizes of material except that it provides for the proper alignment of the top and bottom wheels. Wood is used for some parts because it is cheap and fast to work. The bonus is that it helps to create a vibration-free machine.

I didn't find the right sizes of steel in my scrap piles and so the main platen support is made of wood. I guess that's all right because I used wood for Red's Extendo bracket and idler/tracker arm. Note the bracket made

The 2 by 48 setup.

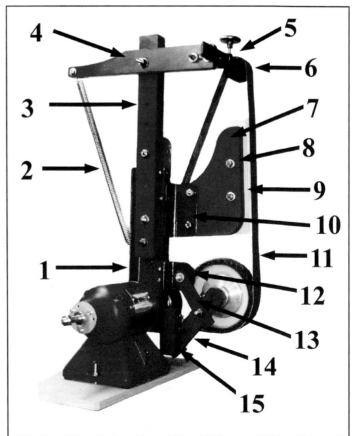

Big Red with a platen and all his parts numbered.

of angle steel (#10 in the illustration), this gives added adjustment to align the platen from front to back. Fine-tuning the platen alignment side-to-side is done with washers at the mounting points.

Finally, a visitor to my shop asked me why I had names for all my machines. I replied that it keeps me from having to say, "...that thing over there" when referring to one of them.

Belt Grinder Tricks And Techniques

As described earlier, the primary purpose of my basic homemade grinder is flat and square grinding. It becomes 500 percent more useful because of the many attachments I've made to use with it. They were developed to make my work easier and more accurate; I couldn't do without them. The attachments eliminate many of the "accidents" I have during the course of making a knife. The attachments make it possible to keep the item being ground in the proper position with the wheel or platen. Other attachments put the work in a position so that I can see what I'm doing. If I can't see what I'm doing I will end up grinding off stuff that should have been left on the blade or handle.

Square Grinding Jig For Detail Work

The inside of a folding knife spring is always a challenge to grind and finish because it's hard to keep the inside surface square with the sides. I made a clamp on table for my three-wheel detail machine that holds parts at exactly 90 degrees to the contact wheel. You can see that set up earlier in this section. I use it with wheels from 1/2 inch to 2 inches in diameter.

Hollow Grinding With A Shaped Platen

The photo shows the position of a 16-inch hollow grinding platen jig. It is shaped of wood and faced with the cork/graphite canvas platen material that most knifemakers' supply companies sell. I have another that will do a 20-inch hollow grind. The platen material will last through one or more knives. I'm not ready to recommend this method for production hollow grinding but for the occasional extra large one it works just fine. The hollow grinding jig is clamped to the flat platen with an ordinary "C" clamp.

The canvas/cork/graphite platen material is available from most knifemaker supply firms.

Slack-Belt Grinding

My basic platen machine has a short slack belt section below the platen and a longer one above. The difference in the length of the slack belt section gives two options on the degree of curvature that can be ground. I have an attachment that clamps in place above the platen that gives me a slack belt space that is about 1-1/2 inches wide; it works great for the convex grind on small and narrow blades.

Convex Grinding Platens

About fifteen years ago I was fighting to get the convex even on a Bowie knife with a 15-inch long blade that was 2-1/2 inches wide. I could not keep the correct tension on the belt and the grind kept changing. I got an idea to make a shaped platen to push the blade into. I made a jig out of wood faced with cork/graphite platen material. It makes the convex grind exactly the same every time until it starts to wear. The graphite material wears on the outer edges first but can be made to last somewhat longer by draw-filing it to get it level. I usually rough the blade in with the flat platen, then mount the convex jig with a fresh piece of canvas/graphite glued in position. I can usually do two large blades without changing the platen material.

The convex jig is held in place on the top platen support with a "C" type ViseGrip® clamp. I have four different jigs that span everything from 1-inch-wide to 3 inches. The jigs are fairly simple to make. The hard part may be to find a way to mount them on a commercial machine with a cast frame. The frame of my upright machine is purposely made of channel, angle and bar steel so there are lots of places to clamp attachments.

Slip-On Platens

When finish grinding with a fine belt on a hard platen the splice going by bumps the blade or handle material and leaves a mark. I have several slip-on platens that use a cushion of carpet behind the grinding surface to smooth out the bump. It works like a charm. The cushion is a piece of indoor/outdoor carpet that is faced with the graphite platen material that is glued to a piece of thin aluminum formed so that it slips over the fixed platen. One of these cushion platen plates has a work area that is only 1-inch-wide and it has a slight radius on it. There are times when this is the only way I can put a fine finish on something. I

This is the hollow-grinding jig that is a substitute for a 16-inch contact wheel. I also have one for a 20-inch circle.

The convex grinding jig in place, also note the belt bumper in place against the edge of the abrasive belt.

have a riser block for the square table that brings the work up and in line with the cushioned surface.

Dovetail Jigs

I have several dovetail jigs; the one I use on my folding knife bolsters is fixed at 30 degrees, another one fixed at 45 degrees, and one that is adjustable. In use, the jigs are clamped to the square table.

The Belt Bumper

It is very frustrating to have a belt that won't track straight. With the finer grits a wobbly belt can undercut the termination point where the grind stops. I call my solution to this problem the "Belt Bumper." I made it by silver-brazing a piece of tungsten carbide to a scrap of angle iron and set it up so that it can be swung over against the side of the platen. The belt is tracked over against the carbide and this will straighten out all but the very worst of heavy, crooked belts.

The Belt Doctor

It's not a bad idea to take a look at a new belt before mounting it on the grinder. See if the splice looks right and check the whole back of the belt for gobs of glue or grit. Wiping the loose grit off the back of new belts before running them the first time can extend platen life.

With a new belt on the grinder I will stand to one side as the belt starts up. If there is an excessive amount of wobble or a crooked splice the belt will be returned to the supplier for replacement with a good one.

Some butt-splice belts have a layer of grit over the joint and that makes a bump as the belt goes past the work. Take a piece of grinding wheel or the edge of a coarse sharpening stone and grind the grit carefully down to the backing. A belt so treated will make less of a bump as the splice goes by.

Belts will last longer without plugging up if given a shot of water from a spray bottle every so often. The eraser type belt cleaner's work to a degree but won't clean a belt clogged with oily wood residue. There are rotary wire brush belt dressers that work pretty well. I'm too cheap to buy one so I use the corner of an old wire wheel to clean clogged belts.

The corner on coarse roughing belts is too square to make a nice transition where the grind leaves off. Use a piece of tungsten carbide or a piece of grinding wheel to round off the corner of the belt.

The Dream Machine

I've shown you two types of belt grinders; two-wheel and three-wheel machines. Then Big Red came along and showed us he can do a lot of different setups. However, he may be overcomplicated. I think I have finally solved the problem of how to make one homemade machine that will do it all and keep it relatively simple. I've got the dimensions worked out on cardboard, complete with the pivot points and all. I even have cardboard wheels that I can set a belt on in order to check the dimensions.

The trick to making a simple but versatile machine comes in two parts. The first is to make the main upright so that it can be quickly lowered to the position where the three-wheel setup can be made. The second is to make the platen attachment quick detachable with the same holding mechanism to grab the wheel-out-front set up.

So, here is the sequence, starting with the platen set up in place:

Remove the belt and take out the platen assembly B.

Lower the main support (A) to the pre set position.

Insert the three-wheel assembly (D) and adjust for the diameter of wheel being run.

Replace the belt and go to work.

Jig for grinding a 30-degree dovetail.

The Flat Disc Grinder

Belt grinders are extremely good at removing metal and getting things relatively flat. They do not have the ability to create a fit that is visibly perfect. Perfect fits are possible with a flat-disc grinder with a foot switch and a medium-fine abrasive in place.

When a belt or disc is moving it is nearly impossible to apply a piece of material to it and then remove it and not round off the edges. That is why a foot switch is essential. Material to be flattened is applied to the disc while it is not moving and then the foot switch is operated. When sufficient material has been removed the foot switch is turned off but the material is not removed until the disc stops turning. This gets the material flat like no other way I've found.

My homemade disc machine is 8 inches in diameter, which is a convenient size to work with. 3-M Spray Disc Adhesive is used to hold ordinary wet or dry paper in place. I cut the discs 8 inches square place them on the machine and then trim off the corners with a sharp knife. The strips of leftover paper are used for hand sanding.

Note the quick-adjustable square table that has been swung out of the way in the picture. In place is a 30-degree dovetail fixture. Note the splashguard and white residue on the machine. I'd been wet-grinding pearl shell shortly before the photo was taken. The base and frame are steel scrap from my collection. The arbor and disc are manufactured to be used together and were purchased at a local lapidary supply. The disc has to run dead true or else flatness cannot be achieved. The machine runs well with a 1/3-hp motor because the disc rpm (800) is low and the cuts are light.

Craig Morgan built the good-looking double disc machine. And, you're wondering where the other disc is; it was on back order at the time the photo was taken. When completed it will have adjustable worktables on both sides.

The advantage of the double disc is that the work is always in the same position, edge up or edge down. With a single disc there is a disadvantage when the disc is turning into the edge.

The 9-inch discs were purchased from Texas Knifemakers Supply. The shaft, bearings and motor were obtained locally. The advantage of a 9-inch disc is that standard sandpaper can be used.

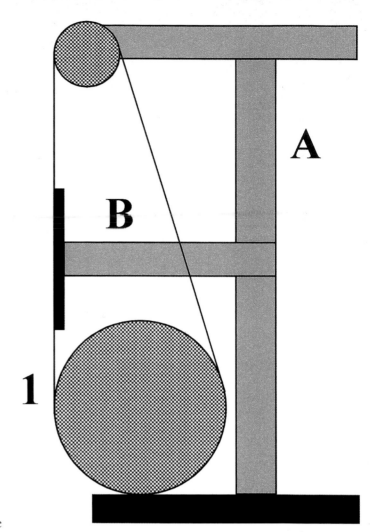

The Dream Machine set up as a platen grinder.

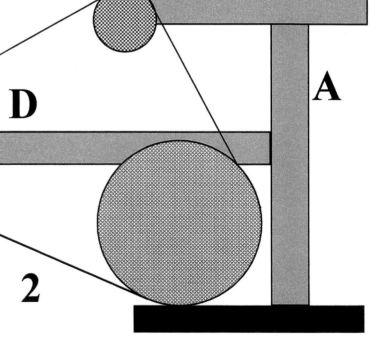

The Dream Machine set up as a hollow-grinding machine, or alternately as a detail machine with smaller wheels.

The homemade flat-disc grinder.

A real nice homemade double disc machine. (Missing disc on back order.)

CHAPTER 8

JIGS, FIXTURES AND HOLDING DEVICES FOR THE KNIFE SHOP

"Oops!" That's a word you don't want to hear while in surgery, or in the knife shop. There are things that can go wrong during the knifemaking process and those "hazards" will always be there. However, there are some good defenses against having to say the "O" word.

The author's work bench. Note the horizontal Wilton vise at the right side of the picture. The height and position make it very handy for a wide variety of gripping operations. The #1 vise is at the bottom left side. The third hand holding device is in the middle and mounted on a Micarta extension to the workbench. I have a variety of work surfaces that I mount to the Micarta extension.

The 3 inch Craftsman with the broken clamp, now repaired and shown in the "vise-in-a-vise" mode.

I've analyzed the numerous "oops" incidents in my career and the majority can be traced to one of three situations. The number one cause happens when I lose my concentration for a moment and stick a part of the knife into a metal-removal operation where it wasn't supposed to be stuck. Another day it may be part of your body that tangles with an abrasive belt, bandsaw blade or drill bit. The number two cause of such incidents is when I thought I could see what I was doing but was mistaken. It is only after the damage is done that the lack of visual accuracy is noticed and by then it's too late to make a correction. Number three on my list of oops causes happens when I lose control of the workpiece. The blade, handle material or whole knife can get out of control.

Having the proper jig or fixture available can eliminate a lot of the risk in the work we do. Even though the proper jig or fixture will help solve problems #2 and #3, you're on your own with #1. In order to do your best work and stay safe it is necessary to work with a clear mind. The "clear

mind" part involves getting some rest when fatigue sets in.

You'll see that many of my jigs are made of Micarta. That's because I have a lot of it that was acquired as industrial scrap, often at no more expense than wood. Good quality hardwood or plywood will work for many of the jigs, use whatever you have on hand.

The Vise

It was 1963 and there wasn't any money available for knifemaking tools. All I had was the homemade Good News Grinder and a used electric drill that had been given to me. As I described earlier in this book, my first workbench was a bookcase.

I didn't have a vise and that led to my first injury as a knifemaker. I was holding a piece of plastic handle material with my left hand and was drilling a hole in it with an electric hand drill. As the bit broke through the backside it grabbed the plastic, which spun in my hand. I had numerous cuts from the plastic and a small hole in

This set of inserts is made of half-inch thick Micarta and are used for gripping a wrapped blade. In this picture a pressure fitted guard is being driven onto the tang.

Inserts for the vise jaws are necessary to protect the work being held from being marked up or dented. This set is made of 1/4 inch Micarta with sole leather glued to the gripping surface.

the palm of my hand from the tip or the drill bit. That was a good lesson in how not to do it, but it wasn't long until I had my first real vise. My sweet wife Phyllis went to Sears and came home with a 3-inch clamp-on vise. ($9.95 was a major investment for us back in 1963.) That little Craftsman vise served me well for several years until I found a good used 4-inch vise.

More than 30 years ago I broke the clamp part off of the little Craftsman by over tightening it. I used two machine screws to attach it to a piece of Micarta and have been using it every since as a vise-in-a-vise. I find it handy for doing filework and fitting guards because it gets the work into the close range of my trifocals.

Consider mounting your most-used vise at a 45-degree angle to the bench. The exception to this is if you have one end of your workbench clear and can mount the vise there. The angled mount allows working from the end of the jaws and also from the side. It will be necessary to use a piece of steel or plywood in order to mount the vise with sufficient clearance for the handle. Note the photo in Chapter 1 that shows a bird's-eye view of my most-used vise. You'll notice that notches have been cut in the jaws so that a knife can be gripped with a trial pin in place.

I must have a dozen different sets of vise jaw inserts. Inserts of Micarta, Micarta lined with leather and Delrin are used to protect blades and handle materials from damage by the steel jaws. I recently made a set with a lip on each side, just the thing for holding a sharpening stone. Other inserts are used for straightening blades. A warped blade that is selectively hardened or tempered can easily be straightened with a three-point set-up in a vise.

The three-point brass pin setup for straightening blades.

Two versions are shown; one has brass pins for the contact point, the other Micarta contact points.

The Rotary Knife Vise

Lloyd Hale brought a rotary vise to the Knifemakers Guild Shows in 1974. It was made out of pipe and pipe fittings and I liked the idea well enough that I soon made my own version. I used a thick piece of Micarta for the body with a steel tube held by steel collars. The internal parts are hardwood with a brass insert where the lock screw tightens the jaws on the knife blade.

An easy-to-construct knife vise can be made of square tube. See the two views of one I made as an experiment. I was just thinking that with a set of vise jaw inserts with a 90-degree "V" on each side it would give access to the handle being detailed in 45-degree increments. That's almost as good as having 360-degrees rotation available.

The Third-hand Holding Device

At the time of my carpal tunnel surgery I had the left hand done first because it had more damage. I was curious as to why the left hand was worse than the right. My surgeon explained that a right-handed craftsman uses the left hand as a vise. The left hand is tightly gripping some part while the right is doing the easy work of carving, filework or polishing.

Arthritis is limiting the use of my left hand. At times my thumb does not want to do what I ask of it. I'm taking the approach that what I have left in the bad hand should be conserved. With that in mind I've spent the last two years developing a holding device that will eliminate most hand gripping of materials being worked on. I call my invention the "third hand".

The project started when I found a #50 Pony clamp in the free box at a yard sale. I hooked it to a piece of Micarta and started using it as a vise-in-a-vise. It soon had soft jaws and a "V" block for holding round handle materials. That simple start soon evolved to a homemade ball joint, then to using two "adjusto" brackets and finally to the "L" shaped bracket shown in the photo. I can see the third hand continuing to evolve and doing its job of saving my left hand from any more repetitive stress damage.

Jigs For Working with Pin Stock

I'm "old school" when it comes to attaching slab type handles. I started out using pins and have stayed with it for 43 years. Not that there is anything wrong with bolt sets or mosaic pins, it's just not my style.

The pin stock gripper is essential because it makes forming a rivet type head on pin stock of your choice. It's easy to make out of any medium to heavy angle iron. Cut two pieces of the angle iron approximately 3" in length and clean up the outer surfaces and make sure the clamping surfaces are flat. Place a business card between the two pieces and clamp them securely together with the top flats in alignment. Drill a series of holes that are the same size of pin stick you want to clamp. The drill point will follow the cardboard and leave half the diameter of the hole minus the thickness of the card on each side of the jig. This allows a tight grip on pin stock that is the same diameter as the drill bit. A head can then be formed with a ball end hammer. This is especially useful when pinning stag and the placement for the pin ends up in the bottom of a groove. You will need to practice some to get a nice even head.

The headed pin stock can be driven into the swage block to create the cone to fit into a countersink in the handle material. The swage block is made of hardenable steel that is drilled, countersinks made, then hardened and tempered to a spring temper. A very shallow counter sink is all that is required.

A specially shaped anvil is used to hold the headed pin stock into the groove in a stag handle. Note the specially shaped hammer with the ball face.

Drill Press Jigs

A blade holder allows the blade to be clamped securely to the jig, which cannot spin on the table because the far end is placed against the column.

A three-point blade straightening setup made of Micarta and angle iron.

Plumb bob /with bottom locator pin. This setup allows the drilling of a through hole in handle material that is longer than the bit and centered on the ends. A plumb bob is used to locate a centering pin that is secured to the table. The center of each end of the handle material is marked and spotted with a small drill bit. One end of the handle material is centered on the locating pin and the other is drilled to half the length of the handle or slightly more. The handle material is then reversed and drilled until the drill meets the hole. This results in a perfectly aligned hole.

The handle-grabbing jig keeps the material being drilled from spinning out of one's grip. This one is made of oak, but almost anything will work.

A friend was moving his machine shop and asked me if I wanted to dig around in his scrap pile. I found some real nice junk and one piece became what I call a side drill jig. It's a box made of machined steel, perfectly square and it works perfectly for holding a narrow tang handle for drilling the tapered hole. The tang is drawn in pencil on the handle blank, which is then clamped to the side of the jig at the correct angle and the spindle stop set. Two setups are required to make the tapered tang hole. One side is drilled, then the handle material adjusted to the angle on the other side of the hole. The brad point drills work the best for this type drilling. They have less of a tendency to wander in the hole. They allow some cutting to be done with the outer edge when enlarging the hole, or blending in the two holes.

Handle Gluing Jig

I tried several highly complicated clamping systems but none of them worked as well as this simple jig. Two pieces of hardwood are shaped and drilled for 5/16-inch all-thread. Make the jig wide enough for the widest blade you will be making. Set up the all-thread with an inch or so of excess on each side, which allows the rubber bands to be stretched over them.

The sequence for the handle shown is as follows. The blade is wrapped with toilet paper and masking tape, the guard is affixed and the spacer epoxied in place. Once the epoxy is cured the jig is clamped to the blade at the proper angle and the rubber bands adjusted so that the crown is pulled up square against the spacer. Some adjustment of the angle the jig pulls at may be necessary. Once the setup is correct the crown is epoxied in place. I don't trust epoxy completely so I always put one pin through the crown.

A blade is completely finished except for sharpening prior to installing the guard and handle. It needs to have a protective sleeve and here's how to do it. Step one is a double layer of toilet paper, paper towel or other. Leave ¼" of the blade clear of the paper.

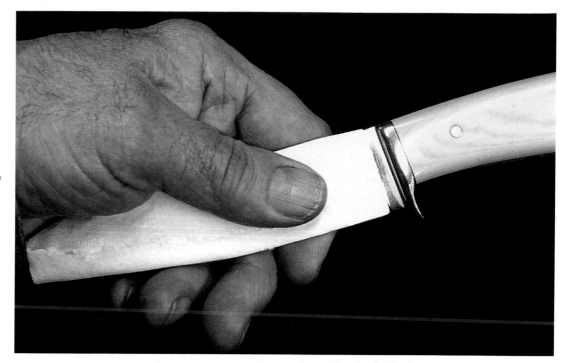

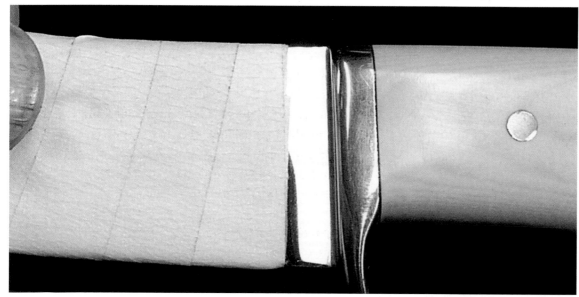

Step two is a wrap of masking tape that stops where the paper wrap ends. At this point the protective sheath will slide off and on the blade.

The final step is a double wrap to cover the bare section of blade, which seals the opening. This step is extremely important because nothing is uglier than a nicely finished blade that gets marked up by grit pressed into the blade by the vise jaws.

The rotary knife holding vise makes handle detailing easy by allowing 360-degree access to the handle being detailed. Look through a scrap yard to find one steel tube that will just slide into another and this will be the start. Or, do like I did on this one back in 1976 and machine a piece of Micarta for a sliding fit for the tube. The internal gripper parts are wood backed up with Micarta.

The rotary vise in the upright position for detailing the butt of the knife handle.

Note that the blade is held in a vise to keep the tang upright. The crown antler piece is epoxied in place with the rubber bands adjusted to keep a snug fit on everything as the epoxy cures.

This is a homemade knife holder that is fairly simple to make using a 2 to 3-inch piece of square tube. The internal blade gripper parts are Micarta.

The square knife holder is in the vertical/angled position.

The two "adjusto" joints can be placed between the base and body thus allowing every angle you could ever think of.

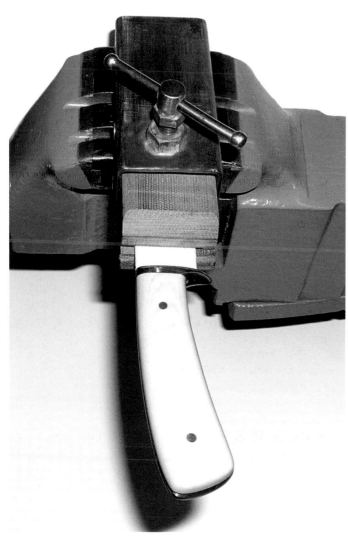

The square knife holder is in the horizontal position

Crown Folder Jigs and Fixtures

I sawed a deer antler in half back in 1968 but soon got discouraged in turning it into a folding knife… I finally finished that first crown folder in 1977. I had to get into folders as a specialty and get several hundred under my belt before I had sufficient "folder smarts" to get the job done. The crown folders became one of my specialties and over the years I've had to develop a variety of jigs and fixtures to take the guesswork out of drilling and sawing the odd-shaped antler pieces.

Getting the crowns off of the whole antler is fairly simple because I've got the main branch of the antler to hang onto. Once the crown is isolated it becomes a bit of

Basic parts layout for the third hand holding device. Note the two pins that locate the "V" block in the base piece. The black Micarta piece slips out when using the "V" block.

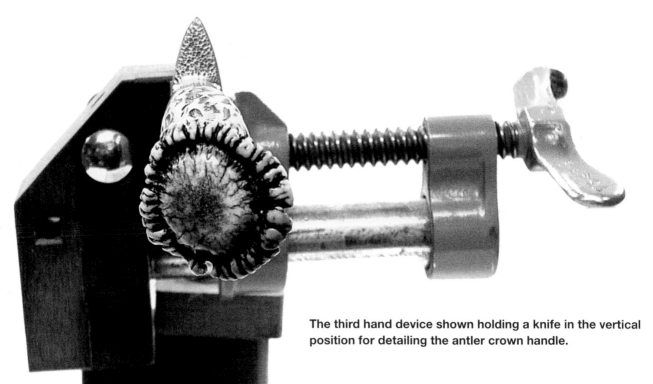

The third hand device shown holding a knife in the vertical position for detailing the antler crown handle.

The third hand with the "V" block holding an antler crown for detailing.

The jig is tipped 90-degrees for working the handle in the horizontal position.

The pin gripper.

The swage block showing the head formed by driving it into the block.

The pin stock in locked in place and ready for heading.

The specially shaped riveting hammer is resting on the anvil which is used to support the pin in the groove on a stag slab while the top side is being riveted. This little anvil was made out of a discarded punch-press punch.

Close up view of the formed head.

a problem. The bandsaw blade has the tendency to spin a hand-held round part out of the grip. After nearly getting pulled into the bandsaw on several occasions I made the "V" block holder shown in the photo. It works extremely well for getting the final trim cut made and also for processing the round sections of elk antlers.

I like to make crown folders where the button is intact. The problem is how to hold the irregular-shaped piece of antler to partially slot it. However, getting the slot cut in a straight line is only part of it. A hole for the blade pivot pin must be drilled and kept square with the slot. Here's my procedure:

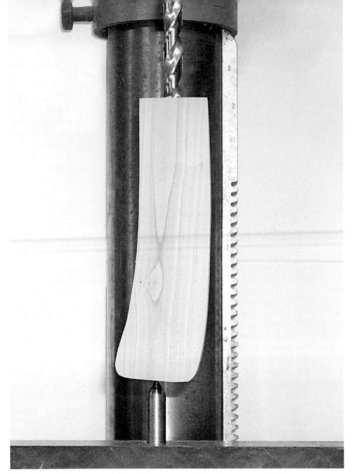

The handle material in alignment for through drilling.

The handle grabber in working mode. The inset shows a brad point drill bit, which is the best type to use for drilling through wood or stag handles.

The side drill jig in use. The object is to drill out the marked section to fit the tang.

1) Draw a pencil line on the crown where the slot is going to be.
2) Use the bandsaw freehand to make a cut on the line approximately 1 1/2-inches into the crown.
3) Clamp the crown to the saw jig with the partial slot tight against the thin band saw material.
4) Carefully cut the slot, stopping just short of the button. You're not cutting the finished width of the slot, just the thickness of the saw cut.
5) Drill the pivot hole using another piece of thin bandsaw material to locate it on the drill press riser.
6) Mount the crown in the jig that looks like a little racecar from the side view. Two machine screws ground to a point locate on the pivot hole to hold the antler at a 90-degree angle for the operation to finish the slotting operation. You'll have to use some leather shims and perhaps put a wedge under the back end of the hold down in order to get the antler tight in the jig. Note the view from the front end of the jig.

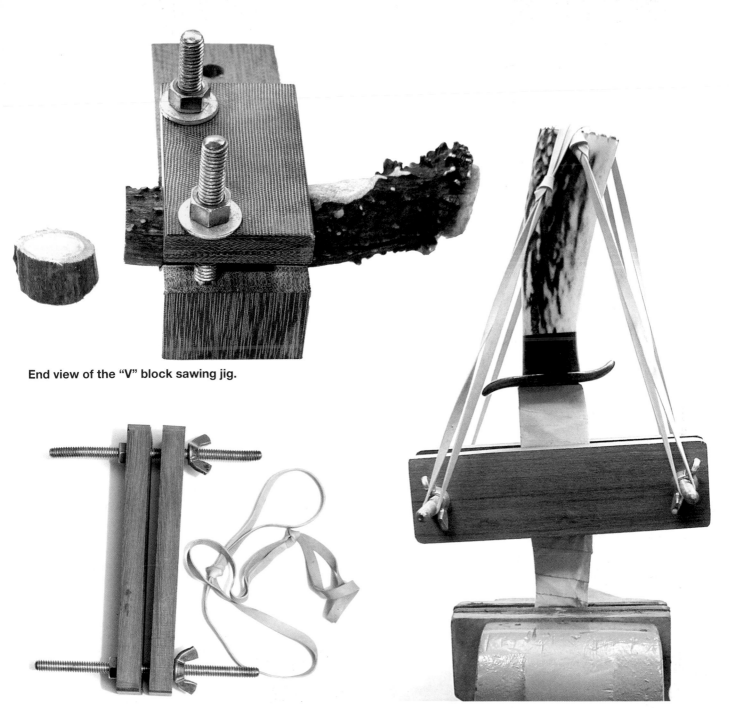

End view of the "V" block sawing jig.

The narrow-tang, handle-gluing jig. Wood, all thread, nuts, washers, wing nuts and rubber bands…..very high tech.

"The knife in the jig has a pommel cap that is screwed on, it wouldn't need the jig for the glue-up. (It was the only knife I had on hand to put in the jig for the photo.}"

7) Use a milling machine or abrasive wheel on a bench grinder to complete the slot.

I call the next crown jig the upside-down drilling fixture. A piece of 1/8-inch steel is mounted to a riser shaped as seen in the photo. The half crown is ground flat on the inside surface and then clamped to the bottom of the steel plate for drilling of the holes for pins. When the first half is drilled it is clamped to the other half and the drill bit is used to start a very shallow hole at the pivot end. The so-marked half is then clamped to the jig and the pivot hole drilled. The two halves are then arranged on the fixture with a trial pin through the pivot hole. (The drilled half on top, the one to be drilled on the bottom of the steel plate.) The two halves are carefully lined up, clamped to the jig and drilled using the first side as a drill jig.

The upside-down fixture is also used to locate the slotted type for counter-boring for the bird's-eye washers.

The upside-down drilling jig.

I don't have a good name for this jig so let's call it a bandsaw jig. It's a thin piece of band saw steel stuck in a piece of wood at a 90-degree angle. It holds an antler crown for additional cutting.

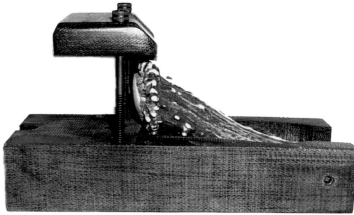

Side view of the slotting jig.

A crown handle piece clamped in the bandsaw jig and partially sawn.

The setup for drilling the pivot hole in a slotted crown handle.

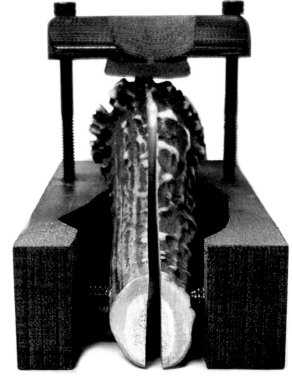

End view of the slotting jig.

Tempil°
Basic Guide to Ferrous Metallurgy

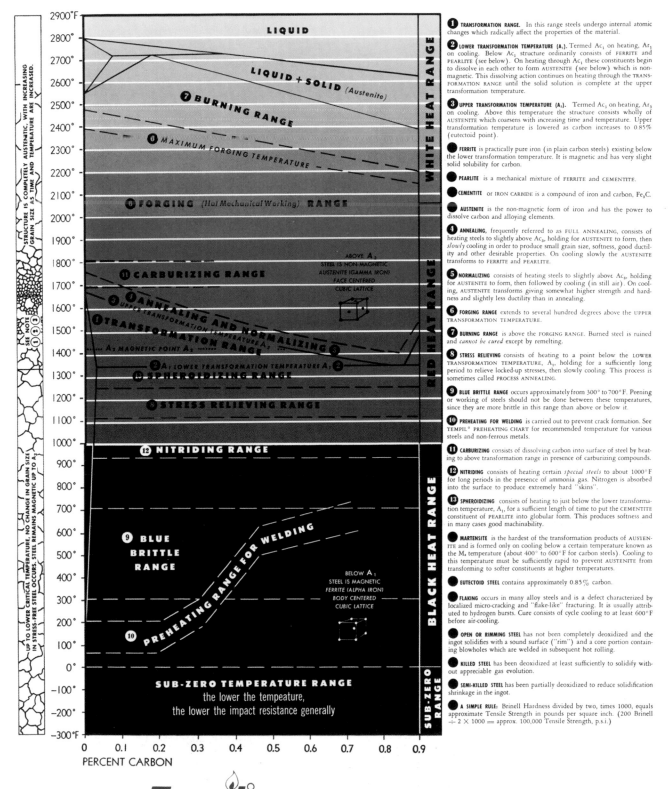

1 TRANSFORMATION RANGE. In this range steels undergo internal atomic changes which radically affect the properties of the material.

2 LOWER TRANSFORMATION TEMPERATURE (A_1). Termed Ac_1 on heating, Ar_1 on cooling. Below Ac_1, structure ordinarily consists of FERRITE and PEARLITE (see below). On heating through Ac_1 these constituents begin to dissolve in each other to form AUSTENITE (see below) which is non-magnetic. This dissolving action continues on heating through the TRANSFORMATION RANGE until the solid solution is complete at the upper transformation temperature.

3 UPPER TRANSFORMATION TEMPERATURE (A_3). Termed Ac_3 on heating, Ar_3 on cooling. Above this temperature the structure consists wholly of AUSTENITE which coarsens with increasing time and temperature. Upper transformation temperature is lowered as carbon increases to 0.85% (eutectoid point).

● FERRITE is practically pure iron (in plain carbon steels) existing below the lower transformation temperature. It is magnetic and has very slight solid solubility for carbon.

● PEARLITE is a mechanical mixture of FERRITE and CEMENTITE.

● CEMENTITE or IRON CARBIDE is a compound of iron and carbon, Fe_3C.

● AUSTENITE is the non-magnetic form of iron and has the power to dissolve carbon and alloying elements.

4 ANNEALING, frequently referred to as FULL ANNEALING, consists of heating steels to slightly above Ac_3, holding for AUSTENITE to form, then *slowly* cooling in order to produce small grain size, softness, good ductility and other desirable properties. On cooling slowly the AUSTENITE transforms to FERRITE and PEARLITE.

5 NORMALIZING consists of heating steels to slightly above Ac_3, holding for AUSTENITE to form, then followed by cooling (in still air). On cooling, AUSTENITE transforms giving somewhat higher strength and hardness and slightly less ductility than in annealing.

6 FORGING RANGE extends to several hundred degrees above the UPPER TRANSFORMATION TEMPERATURE.

7 BURNING RANGE is above the FORGING RANGE. Burned steel is ruined and *cannot be cured* except by remelting.

8 STRESS RELIEVING consists of heating to a point below the LOWER TRANSFORMATION TEMPERATURE, A_1, holding for a sufficiently long period to relieve locked-up stresses, then slowly cooling. This process is sometimes called PROCESS ANNEALING.

9 BLUE BRITTLE RANGE occurs approximately from 300° to 700° F. Peening or working of steels should not be done between these temperatures, since they are more brittle in this range than above or below it.

10 PREHEATING FOR WELDING is carried out to prevent crack formation. See TEMPIL° PREHEATING CHART for recommended temperature for various steels and non-ferrous metals.

11 CARBURIZING consists of dissolving carbon into surface of steel by heating to above transformation range in presence of carburizing compounds.

12 NITRIDING consists of heating certain *special steels* to about 1000° F for long periods in the presence of ammonia gas. Nitrogen is absorbed into the surface to produce extremely hard "skins".

13 SPHEROIDIZING consists of heating to just below the lower transformation temperature, A_1, for a sufficient length of time to put the CEMENTITE constituent of PEARLITE into globular form. This produces softness and in many cases good machinability.

● MARTENSITE is the hardest of the transformation products of AUSTENITE and is formed only on cooling below a certain temperature known as the M_s temperature (about 400° to 600° F for carbon steels). Cooling to this temperature must be sufficiently rapid to prevent AUSTENITE from transforming to softer constituents at higher temperatures.

● EUTECTOID STEEL contains approximately 0.85% carbon.

● FLAKING occurs in many alloy steels and is a defect characterized by localized micro-cracking and "flake-like" fracturing. It is usually attributed to hydrogen bursts. Cure consists of cycle cooling to at least 600° F before air-cooling.

● OPEN OR RIMMING STEEL has not been completely deoxidized and the ingot solidifies with a sound surface ("rim") and a core portion containing blowholes which are welded in subsequent hot rolling.

● KILLED STEEL has been deoxidized at least sufficiently to solidify without appreciable gas evolution.

● SEMI-KILLED STEEL has been partially deoxidized to reduce solidification shrinkage in the ingot.

● A SIMPLE RULE: Brinell Hardness divided by two, times 1000, equals approximate Tensile Strength in pounds per square inch. (200 Brinell ÷ 2 × 1000 = approx. 100,000 Tensile Strength, p.s.i.)

Tempil°
DIVISION, AIR LIQUIDE AMERICA CORP.
2901 Hamilton Blvd., South Plainfield, NJ 07080

GLOSSARY OF TERMS USEFUL FOR KNIFEMAKERS

ALLOY STEEL: An iron-based mixture is considered to be an alloy steel when manganese is greater than 1.65 percent, silicon over 0.5 percent, copper above 0.6 percent, or other minimum quantities of alloying elements such as chromium, nickel, molybdenum, or tungsten are present.

ANNEALING OR FULL ANNEALING: Heating steels to slightly above the upper transformation temperature, holding for AUSTENITE to form then slowly cooling in order to produce a small grain size, softness, good ductility and other desirable properties. On slow cooling the austenite transforms to ferrite and pearlite. (See the Tempil© chart.)

AUSTEMPERING: A heat-treating process where the blade is quenched in a medium such as molten lead or special salt. The temperature of the quenching medium is maintained below that where PEARLITE is formed but above that where MARTENSITE is formed. The result is a tough yet hard microstructure.

AUSTENITE: The non-magnetic form of iron that has the power to dissolve carbon and alloying elements. Translation: At the hardening temperature the alloying elements are dissolved in the carbon and when cooled sufficiently quickly by the quench, the austenite transforms to MARTENSITE.

AUSTENITIZING: The process of heating a ferrous alloy above the transformation range, (see the Tempil® chart on p. (Insert page here)), in order to form austenite.

BANITE: A structure obtained by the transformation of AUSTENITE at a constant low temperature. Banite is usually the result of AUSTEMPERING.

BILLET: Bladesmiths use the word BILLET to describe the starting and in-process stack of materials when making damascus steel. A not-so-common usage of billet is to describe a bar of steel intended for forging.

BRAZING: To join (metals) by melting nonferrous metals or alloys into the joints at temperatures exceeding 800 degrees F.

BUTT: The end of a knife handle.

BUTT CAP: A metal cap or plate attached at the end of a knife handle.

CARBON: The alloy element that turns iron into steel. Knife steels have from .60 to 2.00 percent carbon by weight.

CARBON STEEL: Steel that has carbon as the major alloy element. Often called "plain" carbon steel.

CARVER HANDLE: A tapered and curved section of stag.

CEMENTITE OR IRON CARBIDE IS A COMPOUND OF IRON AND CARBON. TRANSLATION: That's what steel is, a compound of iron and carbon. Cementite can be hardened

CHOIL: A small cut out area that separates the cutting edge from the tang on a folding knife or from the RICASSO on a fixed-blade knife.

CHROMIUM (CR): An alloying element that is essential for imparting corrosion resistance to steel. An oxide film that naturally forms on the surface of stainless steel is what causes resistance to staining or corrosion. The film self-repairs in the presence of oxygen if the steel is damaged mechanically or chemically.

COBALT (CO): An alloy element added to steel that increases the hot hardness.

COKE: The nearly pure form of carbon that is the result of burning the gas and other impurities out of coal.

CPM: CRUCIBLE PARTICLE METALLURGY, see PARTICLE METALLURGY

CROWN STAG: The part of a deer or elk antler that is attached to the head.

DAMASCUS STEEL: A composite steel made by forge welding layers, wires, precut shapes and or powdered metals. In broad terms, any steel that has a pattern on the surface.

DENDRITE: A full-grown GRAIN or crystal in steel.

DIFFUSION: The movement of atoms within a solution. The net movement is usually from regions of high concentrations to regions of low concentration in order to achieve homogeneity of the solution. Translation: An example of diffusion in steel is commonly called carbon migration. This takes place in forge-welded blades, for example, pattern-welded, chain or wire damascus. Each time the blade is heated carbon atoms move from the high carbon layers into the lower carbon layers. After three welding heats the carbon may be equally distributed throughout the blade. The blade will still show a distinctive pattern because of the difference in trace elements and other alloy elements that do not diffuse.

FERRITE: Practically pure iron (in plain carbon steels) existing below the lower transformation temperature. It is magnetic and has very slight solid solubility for carbon. Translation: Ferrite is the form of steel where the carbon is not in solution in the iron.

FLUX: A cleaning agent used in soldering, brazing and welding. Anhydrous borax is a common flux used in FORGE WELDING.

FORGE WELDING: Joining ferrous metals by heating in a forge or furnace. Once the material being heated reaches the welding temperature they are hammered to bring all parts together.

FORGING: The shaping of metal with hand hammers, power hammers or presses. The metal is usually heated in order to make it easier to work.

FORGING RANGE: This temperature range extends to several hundred degrees above the upper transformation temperature. Translation: Steel in this temperature range is plastic enough to be shaped by hand hammering, a power hammer, press or rolling mill.

FULL TANG: A knife handle where the tang is the full profile of the handle shape and the two handle pieces (SLABS) are attached, one on each side.

GRAIN: Upon cooling from the liquid state a metal will form cells. A colony of cells delineated by a boundary makes up a single grain. (See DENDRITE.)

HARDENING: The process that increases the hardness of steel. Usually accomplished in knife blades by heating and QUENCHING.

HEAT: In forging, one cycle of heating and hammering is "a heat."

HEAT TREATMENT: Altering the properties of steel by subjecting it to a series of temperature changes. (See QUENCH AND TEMPERING.)

HIGH-CARBON STEEL: Steel with more than 0.30 carbon. Steel suitable for knives will usually have .50 or more carbon by weight, an average would be .95.

HIGH-SPEED STEEL (HSS): A special class of steels that are alloyed to hold their hardness at the high temperatures generated by cutting tools at fast operating speeds. Drill bits, lathe tools, taps and reamers are usually made of HSS. Very few knives are made out of HSS.

IRON (FE): Iron is the most common metal and when alloyed with carbon it becomes steel.

KYDEX®: Thermoplastic sheet manufactured from an acrylic/PVC alloy. Kydex® sheet has very good abrasion resistance and virtually no moisture absorption. It is used for sheaths, sheath liners and holsters.

MANGANESE (MN): This element is necessary to make steel sound when cast and workable by rolling or forging. MANGANESE is not considered an alloy element until it is added in an amount of over .40 percent.

MARTENISTIC: Martenisitic steels have the ability to form the hard transformation product MARTENSITE.

MARTENSITE: The hardest of the transformation products of AUSTENITE and is formed only on cooling below a certain temperature known as the MS temperature (about 400 to 600 degrees F for carbon steels). Cooling to this temperature must be sufficiently rapid to prevent AUSTENITE from transforming to softer constituents at higher temperatures. Translation: The formation of MARTENSITE is the purpose of the QUENCH. Martensite, as quenched, is too brittle to make a good blade. A

successful TEMPERING process softens the martensite to a degree sufficient to give the blade a correct balance of edge-holding ability and strength.

MICARTA: Micarta is one of the strongest materials known to the plastics industry. Since it is so tough, Micarta is given many tasks in industry that would ordinarily be reserved for metals and it just happens to make very excellent knife handles. There are several common types and grades used for knife handle material. Ivory MICARTA is paper and phenolic, grades NEMA X. What the knife world calls linen MICARTA is cotton with phenolic, grades NEMA CE & LE. G-10 is Fiberglas with epoxy, grades NEMA G-10/FR-4.

MOLYBDENUM (MO): An alloying element used as a raw material for some classes of stainless steel. MOLYBDENUM in the presence of CHROMIUM enhances the corrosion resistance of stainless steel.

NICKEL (NI): Provides a high degree of ductility (ability to change shape without fracture).

NARROW TANG: The tang is totally enclosed by the handle material. Sometimes called a stick tang.

NORMALIZING: Heating steels to slightly above the critical temperature, holding for austenite to form, and then followed by cooling in still air. On cooling, austenite transforms giving somewhat higher strength and hardness and slightly less ductility than in annealing. Translation: Forged blades need to be normalized to relieve the stresses created by the pressures and any uneven heating during the forging process. Normalizing puts the steel through the process of recrystallization, which causes a homogeneous structure.

PARTICLE METALLURGY: A process for making steel from specially alloyed powders. The powder is put in large steel cans that are sealed and then compacted by hot isostatic pressing. The compacts are then forged and rolled into bar stock. Crucible Specialty Metals makes two popular particle metallurgy steels, CPM 440-V and CPM 420-V.

PATTERN-WELDED STEEL: A type of Damascus steel that is made by forge welding layers made up of iron and steel; two different types of high-carbon and alloy steel or any of many combinations of dissimilar steel types.

PEARLIT: A mechanical mixture of FERRITE and CEMENTITE. Translation: This is one of the components of steel when it is in the soft form.

POMMEL: A knob or end plate of a sword or knife handle.

QUENCHING: Rapid cooling of MARTENISITIC steels for the purpose of creating the transformation product MARTENSITE. This makes the steel hard and brittle and so is always followed by a TEMPERING process.

QUENCH TEST: Quenching a piece of steel in order to determine its ability to harden.

QUENCHANT: The material used for rapid cooling of the blade during quenching. Water, oil, molten lead and liquid salts are all used as quenchants. The type of quenchant does not matter as much as its ability to extract the heat from the part being quenched. Some steel types require a fast quenchant, others can be quenched in a slower-acting quenchant.

RICASSO: An unsharpened section of a blade that is just ahead of the guard.

ROCKWELL HARDNESS: The standard hardness test for blades is performed by a "Rockwell" test machine. Knife blades are measured with the Rockwell "C" scale. A blade that tested 60 on the "C" scale would be reported as 60 Rc.

SAMBAR STAG: Antler parts from an elk type animal native to India.

SCALE: The oxide of iron that forms on the surface of steel when heated above a certain temperature.

SILICON (SI) AN ALLOY ELEMENT NECESSARY FOR STEEL MAKING AND IN PERCENTAGES GREATER THAN .40 IT HELPS WITH STRENGTH.

SILVER BRAZING: (See BRAZING.) A high-strength brazing process that uses a silver-bearing filler metal. Silver brazing is often called SILVER SOLDERING. Such a usage is incorrect. The two processes are different as classified by temperature ranges according to industry standards.

SILVER SOLDERING: This joining process uses soft solder containing silver. The usual temperature range is approximately 460 degrees F.

SLABS: The handle materials on a full-tang knife.

SOFT SOLDERING: Joining metals with a low-temperature alloy commonly composed of lead and tin.

STEEL: An iron-based metal with carbon as the main alloying element.

STELLITE: A cobalt-based metal available in several different grades. The most common grade used for knives is 6K.

STOCK REMOVAL: The blade-making method where saws, grinders and even milling machines are utilized to shape the blade. Forged blades are usually shaped to within 80 to 90 percent of the finished size and then the stock-removal method is used to finish them.

STAINLESS STEEL: A broad class of steels that are alloyed to be stain resistant. The alloy element that imparts stain resistance is chromium. Knife steels that are stainless usually have a minimum of 14 percent chromium.

TALONITE®: A cobalt-based metal that is similar to Stellite 6B.

TEMPERING: A softening and stress-relieving operation that is usually the final step in the heat-treating sequence. Tempering temperatures run from 350 degrees F up to 975 degrees F.

TITANIUM (TI): Titanium is used as a cleaning and deoxidizing agent in molten steel, and when alloyed with aluminum and other metals it is used for folding knife parts such as the sides or locking liner.

TOOL STEELS: A special class of alloy steels that are designated by a letter/number system. W-1, A-2, D-2 and M-4 are examples of tool steels.

TUNGSTEN (W): When first discovered it was called Wolfram. Tungsten is an important alloy element in HIGH-SPEED STEELS.

VERMICULITE: A soft, hydrous silicate mineral used as an insulating material for annealing .

WELDING: To unite (pieces of metal, plastic, etc.) by heating until molten and fused or until soft enough to hammer or press together

ZYTEL®: A nylon resin product that includes modified and unmodified nylon homopolymers and copolymers plus modified grades produced by the addition of heat stabilizers, lubricants, ultraviolet screens, nucleating agents, tougheners, reinforcements, etc. The common ZYTEL® found on knife handles is reinforced with Fiberglas.

I

India stone, 57, 160
Insulation, 21, 24, 160

V

Jack, 39, 115, 160
Japanese, 32, 35-36, 49, 55, 102, 160
Jig, 28, 53-55, 63-64, 85-86, 97, 137-139, 143, 146, 148-150, 152-154, 160

K

Kaowool, 22, 160
Knife board, 14, 17, 19, 102, 160
Kris, 97, 100, 160
Kydex, 157, 160
Lantern, 30, 160
Lathe, 14, 49, 130-132, 135, 157, 160

L

Lawnmower, 5, 19, 50-52, 64, 82, 119, 160
Leather, 13, 34, 50, 58, 63, 73, 89, 102, 144, 153, 160
Liquid Wrench, 121, 160
Lum, Bob, 160

M

Magnet, 19, 70, 72, 75-76, 81, 117, 160
Manganese, 117, 156-157, 160
Manhattan Supply Corporation, 52, 160
Mapp, 24, 28, 160
Martensite, 70-71, 82, 156-158, 160
Masonry, 26, 160
Micarta, 13-15, 58, 66, 131, 135-136, 142-146, 148-149, 157, 160
Mirror, 59-60, 160
Motor, 5, 11, 15, 25, 49-50, 122, 124-126, 128-129, 131-133, 135-136, 140, 160
MSC, 52, 160

N

Narrow tang, 40, 63, 65-66, 146, 157, 160
Neo-Tribal Metalsmiths, 92-93, 160
New Castle, 26, 160
Norizon, 33, 160
Normalized, 40, 42-43, 69, 74-76, 119, 157, 160
Northwest Blacksmith Association, 28, 78, 160
Northwest Safari Cutlery
Rendezvous, 95, 160

O

O-1, 69, 113, 160
Oil, 19, 63, 73-74, 78, 80, 82, 84, 117, 119, 121, 158-160
Oxygen, 24, 34, 36, 46, 83, 106-108, 156, 160

P

Pacific Machinery and Tool Steel, 38, 113, 160
Packing, 25, 36, 74-77, 160
Paco's Fun House, 97, 160
Parker brand, 27, 160
Pattern, 16, 57-59, 100, 108-110, 112-113, 116-117, 121, 156, 160
Pearl Harbor, 130, 160
Peter Wright, 30, 160
Pins, 13, 19, 63, 85, 145, 149, 153, 160
Pits, 36, 160
Platen, 12, 48, 54, 125-126, 128-129, 132, 134-140, 160
Poker, 19, 46, 160
Polish, 55, 59-60, 160
Pommel, 66, 69, 98, 153, 158, 160
Pre-form, 7, 40-42, 97, 99-100, 160
Priest, John, 160
Primitive, 4, 19, 22, 25, 36, 65, 70, 90, 92-93, 95, 97, 102-103, 160
Propane, 19, 21-22, 24-27, 30, 43, 69, 80, 83, 107, 160

Q

Quench, 5, 55, 72-76, 78, 80-84, 94, 97, 117, 119, 156-158, 160
Quenched, 28, 43, 70, 72-75, 78-79, 81-82, 97, 124, 156-158, 160

R

Radio Shack, 121, 160
Rail, 5, 31-33, 160
Railroad, 5, 24, 30-32, 97, 110, 160
Rake, 19, 23-24, 27, 44-45, 60, 96-97, 160
Rasp, 16, 49, 160
RCH, 59, 160
Regulator, 21, 26, 77-78, 160
Regulator block, 77-78, 160
Rider, Dave, 160
Riveted, 68-69, 85, 129, 151, 160
Rockwell, 72, 89, 158, 160
Rope, 23, 46-47, 89, 105, 110, 112-113, 116-119, 160
Rotary, 52, 138, 145, 148, 160

S

Safety glasses, 16, 50, 160
San Mai, 108-110, 160
Sand-blasted, 60, 160
Sandpaper, 19, 34, 37, 42-43, 63, 103, 140, 160
Satin finish, 59-60, 160
Scagel, William, 160
Scale, 19, 34, 36, 46, 53, 74-75, 82, 85, 88, 106-108, 158, 160
Silver, 67-69, 72, 103, 108, 110-111, 158, 160
Slab, 61, 63, 66, 145, 151, 160
Smithy, 6, 12, 20, 26, 44, 72, 79-80, 108, 113, 119, 160
Soak time, 108, 160
Soft back draw, 70, 78, 83, 160
Solder, 69, 158, 160
Sontag, Carl, 160
Spectrographic testing, 116, 160
Spring, 7, 16, 19, 26, 28, 30-31, 37-40, 63-64, 67, 69, 81, 119, 129, 135-137, 146, 160
Square Wheel Grinder, 126, 160
Squirrel cage, 25, 160
Stainless, 15, 28, 38, 59, 72, 75, 80, 82, 85, 93, 109, 156-158, 160
Starrett, 34, 160
Steel wool, 19, 63, 160
Stock-removal, 4-5, 7, 12, 15, 19, 48, 50-51, 56, 60, 63-64, 77, 82, 158, 160
Stone, 16, 33-34, 52, 56-57, 92, 97, 138, 145, 160
Stones, 33, 37, 42-43, 55-57, 92, 97, 160
Straight edge, 43, 160
Stress riser, 67, 160
Swages, 31, 160
Sword, 32, 35-36, 49, 55, 69, 106, 118, 120, 158, 160
Swyhart, Art, 160

T

Table-top forge, 92, 97, 160
Talent, 8, 10, 50, 53, 160
Tallow, 78, 160
Tamping, 119, 160
Tang, 37, 39-40, 42-43, 58, 61, 63-69, 93-94, 98, 144, 146, 149, 152, 156-157, 160
Temper, 49, 55, 67, 69, 82-86, 88, 97, 119, 121, 146, 160
Tempering, 28, 49, 69-70, 72, 74, 78, 82-83, 85-86, 88-89, 94, 96-97, 124, 157-158, 160
Tempering Gizmo, 82-83, 85-86, 96, 160

Testing

Testing, 67, 72, 76, 82, 86, 88-89, 116, 160
Thermal cycles, 76-77, 89, 160
Thermal packing, 76, 160
Thermometer, 74, 78, 160
Thorp, Raymond, 160
Tin-can forge, 22, 160
Toaster oven, 5, 19, 82-83, 85, 160
Tombstone, 33-34, 160
Tongs, 19, 39, 47, 73, 78, 80, 124, 160
Tree branch, 5, 19, 63, 65, 160
Trenton, 30, 160
Turbo torch, 28, 160
Tuyere, 24-25, 45, 160

V

Vacuum, 33, 89, 160
Vanadium, 117, 160
ViseGrip, 60, 85, 96, 137, 160

W

W-1, 158, 160
W-2, 73, 160
Warp, 43, 53, 75, 160
Watco, 64, 160
Wavy, 34, 97, 100-101, 160
WD-40, 63, 121, 160
Wedge, 17, 28, 31, 42, 48-52, 97, 102-103, 153, 160
Welded, 31, 47, 69, 93, 106, 109, 113-116, 118-119, 132, 134, 159-160
Wildcat, 33, 160
Wilton, 15, 126, 135, 142, 160
Wire, 19, 23, 26, 28, 46-47, 67, 73, 85, 102, 105, 107-119, 138, 156, 160
Wire rope, 23, 46-47, 105, 110, 112-113, 116-119, 160
Wood, 13-14, 16-17, 19, 25-26, 30, 32-34, 37, 44-45, 50-51, 58, 60, 62-63, 69, 76, 79, 88, 102, 126, 136-138, 143, 148, 152-154, 160
WorkMate, 94, 97, 160
World's Smallest Forge, 5, 19, 26, 37, 64, 80, 160

Z

Zones, 46, 160

STEEL TYPES

1084, 38, 82, 159
1095, 38, 82, 98, 159
5160, 37-39, 75, 82, 159
52100, 69, 75, 159
9260, 37, 159

INDEX

A

Abrasive, 5, 16, 38, 42-43, 50-51, 57-58, 124-126, 130, 132-133, 136, 138-139, 143, 153, 159
Acetylene, 21, 24, 83, 159
Admiral Steel, 38, 159
Alloway, Tiny, 159
American Bladesmith Society, 42, 72, 87, 159
Annealing, 42, 74-76, 79, 156-159
Anvil, 5, 19, 27-36, 38-40, 42, 76, 89, 94, 96-97, 99, 101, 124, 146, 151, 159
Arc Welded, 69, 159
Ash, 24-25, 45-46, 159
Austentite, 159
Automatic layers, 116, 159

B

Bacon grease, 78, 159
Baldor, 135-136, 159
Bar stock, 15-16, 30, 37-40, 53, 64, 98-100, 158-159
Barbecue, 5, 7, 24-25, 159
Bargain, 103, 125, 159
Bastard File, 55, 159
Belt grinder, 5, 7, 43, 48-49, 57-58, 63, 89, 123-126, 128-130, 136, 159
Belt speed, 54, 129, 159
Bench, 12-14, 30, 34, 38, 49, 60, 124, 132, 142, 144, 153, 159
BernzOMatic, 19, 22, 25-26, 159
Bevel, 5, 34, 36, 40-41, 42-43, 48, 51-52, 54-55, 97, 99-102, 159
Bick, 30-32, 159
Big Red, 132, 134-136, 138, 159
Billet, 15-16, 97, 106-108, 110, 114, 118-119, 156, 159
Birchwood Casey Super Blue, 121, 159
Black, James, 159
Blanks, 5, 50, 159
Blow, 30, 33, 38-39, 42, 44, 76, 99, 01, 159
lower, 19, 21, 24-25, 44-46, 159
rax, 28, 108, 118, 157, 159
, Paul, 159
ie, James, 159
rod test, 72, 86, 88, 159
ng, 61, 67-69, 72, 156-159
26-28, 38, 45, 94, 108, 159

Brine, 73, 159
Bucket, 45, 80, 159
Buffalo skinner, 40, 159
Buffer, 59-60, 159
Buffing compound, 86, 159
Bumper, 39, 137-138, 159

C

Cable, 46, 110, 113-116, 118, 159
Camp knife, 80, 88, 159
Candlewick, 73, 159
Cap, 24, 65-66, 69, 98, 153, 156, 159
Carbon, 30, 38-39, 49, 72, 76, 78, 82, 106, 108, 113, 116-117, 119, 156-159
Carbonizing, 107, 159
Carpet, 60, 137, 159
Center-finder, 53, 159
Chapman, Gene, 159
Cherry, 72, 159
Chromium, 37, 75, 117, 156-159
Classes, 43, 157, 159
Clay, 22, 24, 33, 159
Clinker, 45-46, 159
Coal, 5, 7, 19-21, 24-25, 36-38, 43-47, 67, 107, 113, 118, 156, 159
Coat hanger, 19, 108, 110, 159
Coke, 25, 43, 45-46, 118, 156, 159
Cold blue, 121, 159
Cold-rolled, 75, 159
Columbium, 117, 159
Compound, 59-60, 86, 156, 159
Convex grinding, 137-138, 159
Conveyor, 60, 159
Copper, 49, 63-65, 85-86, 97-98, 126, 156, 159
Critical temperature, 72, 77, 106, 157, 159
Crystal, 72, 76-77, 124, 156, 159
Crystalon, 57, 159
Cutting plate, 31, 159

D

Dagger, 12, 36, 60, 97-102, 111, 114, 117, 159
Damascus, 4, 15-16, 23, 27-28, 38, 67, 102, 104-105, 107-116, 118-119, 121, 156, 158-159
Danish Oil, 63, 159
Dayton, 132, 135, 159
Decarburization, 108, 113, 116, 159
Deft, 63-64, 159
Devcon, 61, 159

Die, 119, 159
Dixie Gun Works, 5, 159
Dragon Breath, 21-22, 26, 159
Drawfiling, 14, 42, 55, 102, 159
Dresser, 52, 159
Drill, 5, 12, 16, 26-27, 50, 52, 61, 63, 74, 92, 128-129, 143-144, 146, 152-153, 157, 159
Drill bits, 16, 157, 159
Drill press, 5, 12, 63, 92, 129, 146, 152, 159
Dumpster, 16, 62-63, 159

E

Edge-quench, 78, 81-82, 159
Epoxy, 61, 63, 69, 121, 148-149, 157, 159
Etch, 121, 159
Etching, 55, 60, 119, 121, 159
Extendo bracket, 136, 159
Extendo Forge, 25-26, 30, 32, 159

F

Fan blades, 25, 159
Ferrule, 28, 63-65, 94, 97, 159
Finish, 12, 14, 34, 36-37, 40, 42-43, 52, 55-61, 63-64, 67, 92, 102, 119, 121, 124, 137, 153, 158-160
Finishing, 4, 34, 42, 48, 55-59, 61, 74-76, 89, 92, 97, 122, 159
Finishing heat, 42, 74-76, 159
Fire, 20-23, 25, 27, 34, 36-37, 39, 43-47, 73, 75, 78, 80-81, 94, 97, 107, 118, 124, 159
Fire clay, 22, 159
Fire hole, 25, 27, 159
Firebrick, 19, 25-26, 28, 38, 80, 159
Fisher, 30, 159
Flame, 19, 22, 24, 27-28, 38, 44-46, 73-74, 78, 80, 83, 107, 159
Flaws, 107-108, 114, 116, 119, 159
Flexibility, 78, 84, 114, 159
Flux, 28, 69, 108, 118, 157, 159
Forge, 5, 7, 14-15, 19-28, 30-32, 34-35, 37-40, 42-43, 45-47, 64, 67, 73-74, 79-80, 83, 85-86, 90-97, 100-102, 106-108, 110, 116-119, 124, 156-160
Forged, 4-5, 7, 10, 14-16, 19-20, 23, 27, 30, 32, 34, 36-37, 39-42, 46, 55-58, 63-66, 69, 74, 76-77, 80-81, 89, 92-93, 95, 97-101, 114, 116, 119, 157-159
Fuller, 28, 31, 39-40, 100, 159

Full-tang, 39, 42, 51, 61, 65-66, 80, 158-159
Furnace cement, 22, 27-28, 159

G

Gas, 20-21, 24, 27-28, 36, 43, 46-47, 67, 69, 79, 83, 107, 110, 118, 156, 159
Gloves, 50, 63, 73, 159
Glue, 13, 59, 88, 132, 138, 159
Goggles, 50, 159
Goo, Tai, 93, 159
Good News Grinder, 50-52, 122-124, 143, 159
Goop, 5, 70, 78-81, 159
Grain, 36, 55, 67-69, 72, 74-77, 117, 124, 156-157, 159
Granite, 33-34, 159
Green Chrome, 59, 159
Green River, 51, 159
Grinder, 5, 7, 11-12, 14, 16, 33-34, 36-38, 42-43, 48-54, 56-58, 63, 89-90, 92, 122-130, 132, 135-136, 138-141, 143, 153, 159-160
Grinding well, 159

H

Hair dryer, 24-25, 37, 159
Hammer, 14, 19, 30-34, 36, 39-40, 42, 66, 74-77, 89, 92, 96-97, 99-101, 106, 110, 117-119, 124, 146, 151, 157-159
Handle, 5, 10, 13, 19, 33, 37, 39, 42, 46-47, 51, 61-69, 85-86, 88, 93-94, 97-98, 102-103, 108, 111, 119, 124, 137, 143-148, 150, 152, 154, 156-159
Hand-rubbed, 5, 52, 55, 57-60, 121, 159
Hand-sanding, 14, 159
Harbor Freight, 72, 159
Hardening temperature, 19, 72-73, 78, 156, 159
Hardie, 28, 31-32, 37-39, 42, 159
Hay-Budden, 30-31, 159
Heat-treatment, 53, 86, 159
High-carbon, 113, 116-117, 157-159
Holford, Henry I., 159
Hollow grinding, 53, 125-126, 130, 137, 159
Holstrom, John Gustaf, 160
Horn, 30-32, 35, 42, 160
Hudson Bay Company, 24, 160